Praise for
Drowning in Screen Time

"David Murrow has a gift for addressing current issues that matter and offering solutions that work. He's done it again with *Drowning in Screen Time*. This book will leave you informed, alarmed, and inspired to take immediate action."

—**RICHARD BLACKABY**, co-author of *Experiencing God* and
Spiritual Leadership

"What if you could wave a magic wand and find an extra twelve hours per week? David Murrow can show you how. Dave was drowning in screen time, got rescued, and recovered an astonishing twelve hours per week. He's become one of America's leading experts on one of the most compelling problems facing this generation and wrote a book!

"*Drowning in Screen Time* is a spectacular *tour de force* that blends parables, data, case studies, stunning personal vulnerability, and so many practical suggestions that there's something here for everyone—parent, teacher, pastor, counselor, gamer, addict, worker—you name it. I highly recommend this book, and if you're a parent, it's must-reading."

—**PATRICK MORLEY, PH.D.**, author of the bestselling book
Man in the Mirror with four million copies in print

"David Murrow digs deep and pulls back the covers to reveal what's really happening when we get lost in our screens. This book is an urgent and needed wake-up call for all who value the soul and deep relationships."

—**KENNY LUCK**, ECPA Platinum Award–winning author,
founder of Every Man Ministries, and author of *Dangerous
Good: The Coming Revolution of Men Who Care*

"If you have teenagers, they have cell phones and computers. If they have cell phones and computers, they are addicted. If they are addicted, you want to help them, and David Murrow has written just the book we need just when we needed it!"

—**BRAD STINE**, stand-up comedian known as "God's Comic"

"I needed this book for my own well-being. With *Drowning in Screen Time*, David Murrow is the Morpheus to our Neo. Take the red pill and read this book today!"

—**TIERCE GREEN**, director of the Authentic Manhood Initiative and co-presenter of *33 The Series*

"I have not met one parent, youth leader, or teacher who doesn't think screen time is one of the major issues of our day. We must figure out how to create a media-safe home. David Murrow has written a well-researched and important book to help us make better decisions and teach our children to do the same."

—**JIM BURNS, PH.D.**, president of HomeWord and author of *Doing Life with Your Adult Children: Keep Your Mouth Shut and the Welcome Mat Out*

"This engaging and easy-to-read book exposes the sinister world of digital entanglement that has taken us all captive—and gives us a way out. *Drowning in Screen Time* is a must-read for every adult, parent, and grandparent. If you want to get back ten years of your life, read this book."

—**REVEREND PAUL LOUIS COLE, D.TH.**, president of the Christian Men's Network

"*Drowning in Screen Time* is a timely book that exposes the hidden dangers lurking in the deep waters of unhealthy, excessive, and addictive screen use. With personal stories, parables, research, and practical principles, David Murrow throws us a lifeline that leads to safety. This insightful book is a lighthouse to a culture that is sinking in a sea of chaos."

—**MICHELLE WATSON CANFIELD, PH.D.**, author of *Let's Talk: Conversation Starters for Dads and Daughters* and Radio/Podcast host of *The Dad Whisperer*

"David Murrow gives us an insider's account of how screens of all kinds are shaping and controlling us, our families, and friends. He then provides simple, practical tips to take back control and live with our screens in healthy ways. You'll find here a reasoned, balanced approach to taming a powerful—and sometimes dangerous—technological phenomenon."

—**THOM SCHULTZ**, founder and president of Group Publishing

"OK, David Murrow, you win. After reading your book, I'm going to do something about all those mindless minutes I've been wasting staring at my screens. Thank you for writing a book that's readable, sensible, and above all, doable."

—**PAUL COUGHLIN**, president of The Protectors: Freedom from Bullying, Courage, Character & Leadership for Life

"As my wife and I raised our four children, we talked often about the dangers of excessive screen time. We did our best to guide them and limit their screen activity. However, looking back, we were not truly equipped nor fully aware of the perils of excessive screen time (nowhere close, actually). David Murrow has done a fantastic job laying out a compelling and practical message of warning people of ALL ages of the dangers of screen time. This book is exceptionally researched and utterly sobering."

—**ROD HANDLEY**, founder and president of Character That Counts

"With the average American spending nine hours a day absorbed in their screens, the need for a book like this one is painfully obvious. Fortunately, the solutions David Murrow offers aren't painful at all. I've begun cutting back on screen time, and I'm happier for it. So are my loved ones."

—**RICK JOHNSON**, bestselling author of *Better Dads, Stronger Sons*

"You only get one life...is this how you want to spend it—staring at screens? Dig into this book and let it set you free."

—**JEFF KEMP**, author of *Facing the Blitz* and retired NFL quarterback for the Seattle Seahawks

"It should be obvious, but until I read David Murrow's book, I hadn't realized that screen time is a two-headed monster. It's not just what we see that affects us—the real problem is how much time we're sacrificing to these glowing time-wasters. This book strengthened my resolve to stay engaged in real life, and I think it will do the same for you."

—**JIM WHITMORE**, president of the National Coalition of Ministries to Men

DROWNING IN SCREEN TIME

DROWNING
IN
SCREEN TIME

DAVID MURROW

SALEM
BOOKS
an imprint of Regnery Publishing
Washington, D.C.

Salem Books™ is a trademark of Salem Communications Holding Corporation
Regnery® is a registered trademark of Salem Communications Holding Corporation

ISBN: 978-1-68451-087-0
eISBN: 978-1-68451-105-1

Library of Congress Control Number: 2020939345

Published in the United States by
Salem Books
An Imprint of Regnery Publishing
A Division of Salem Media Group
Washington, D.C.
www.SalemBooks.com

Manufactured in the United States of America

10 9 8 7 6 5 4 3 2 1

Books are available in quantity for promotional or premium use. For information on discounts and terms, please visit our website: www.SalemBooks.com.

CONTENTS

Section III: I'm Ready to Get My Screen Use under Control

Section IV: I Want to Help Others with Their Screen Use

FOREWORD

A young pastor once asked me if I would mentor him. He was serving at his first church and was experiencing significant difficulties. Upon our first meeting, he had no sooner settled into his seat in my office than his cell phone noisily vibrated, alerting him to an incoming message. I will never forget the look on the man's face. He knew I was a busy person and that my time was valuable. But his curiosity was killing him! So he glanced at his phone for several seconds before returning his attention to me. Less than three minutes later, another notification interrupted our conversation. Again, he looked down at his phone before rejoining our conversation.

"Is anything wrong?" I asked.

"No. Everything's good," he replied.

I had barely resumed speaking when his phone buzzed yet again. At that point, I'd had enough. I told the man I didn't mind talking with him, but I didn't have time to sit and watch him check his messages every few minutes. He got the message. As soon as our meeting was over, he hurriedly made his way to my driveway and sat in his car reading all his missed messages. He eventually left the ministry.

I realized I had witnessed something deeply troubling. The man was facing significant problems he desperately needed to resolve. I was capable of helping him. But the device in his hand seemed determined to control his life. It constantly interrupted him and left him distracted and unfocused. And like a salivating Pavlovian dog, each time he received a new notification, the pastor was gripped with an overpowering compulsion—dare I say, addiction—to reward himself by looking at his device.

We live in a troubled age. People spend hundreds of hours each month engrossed in media when only a generation or two ago they would have invested themselves in something healthier and more productive. The depression and suicide rates among teens, especially females, have reached alarming levels. The current polarization in society is unprecedented. The media industry spends billions of dollars making products as addictive as possible. Now people can "friend" total strangers in the hope they will reciprocate and "friend" them in return. The result? People have thousands of "friends" but no one to call when they have a problem. Or people post updates on Facebook and then anxiously check every few minutes to see if anyone "liked" them. Life is increasingly becoming virtual, and the consequences are disturbing.

I first became aware of David Murrow in 2005 when his bestselling book *Why Men Hate Going to Church* came out. People had sensed for some time that there was a problem with church, but they were uncertain what it was. Murrow drew a bullseye on the issue, and people have been grappling with his insights ever since. Now he is tackling a new problem, and this one is far more powerful, pervasive, and perilous. This book may alarm you. It could disturb you. Hopefully, it will mobilize you.

Many people today behave like the raging alcoholic who adamantly insists he can quit drinking at any time. Like the addict, we know we are in trouble, yet we are so entwined with our media devices that we feel as if we cannot be separated from them. This book is timely. Not only does it identify the problem, but it also offers practical solutions. It's best not to read this book by yourself. You should read it with others who can help you grapple with this extremely complex issue and who may need to help set you free from the sinister media dragons that are determined to enslave you. Read this book carefully and prayerfully and then take action. Before it's too late.

Richard Blackaby
President of Blackaby Ministries International
Co-author of *Experiencing God* and *Spiritual Leadership*

Read Me First

Today is April 27, 2020. At noon I will press "send" and transmit the first draft of this book to my publisher.

My timing couldn't be better—or worse, depending on how you look at it. Billions of people are under stay-at-home mandates, "socially distancing" from one another to slow the spread of the COVID-19 virus. The global economy is buckling. Schools are closed. Freeways are deserted. Airports are empty. Businesses are sliding toward bankruptcy, and millions of workers find themselves suddenly unemployed.

What's holding the world together? Screens.

People are working from home via screen. Children are attending class via screen. Churches are worshipping via screen. Entertainment is pouring into our homes via screen.

"Pouring" is the operative word. "Our family is drowning in screen time," a friend of mine posted on Facebook. "My wife and I work from home via Zoom. Our three kids attend virtual classes on their school-issued laptops. My son spends most of his free time playing video games while my teenage daughters are lost in social media. Everyone is binge-watching TV."

But even before the virus lockdowns confined us to our homes, humanity was drowning in screen time. A pre-virus survey found that the typical American consumes nine hours of screen entertainment each day. Screens have been socially distancing us since they began entering our living rooms in the 1950s.

I write not as an academic but as a man who almost drowned in screen time. I didn't realize I was in over my head, neglecting the important things, and hurting the people I love.

My Journey from Screen Addiction to Freedom

I was born in 1961, just as screens became ubiquitous in American homes. My father bought his first black-and-white TV a few months before I arrived. If we were home and awake, the TV was on. The Murrows started each morning with the *Today* show and fell asleep to *The Tonight Show*. We were the first family on the block to own a VCR—a Betamax purchased for $1,600 in 1977. (That's almost $7,000 in 2020 dollars, adjusted for inflation.)

My father's screen obsession disgusted me. He spent most of his free time absorbed in his TV, avoiding real life. *I'll never do that*, I told myself. I pretty much stopped watching television when I became a teenager. I was proud of myself for conquering Dad's compulsion.

Ironically, I graduated from college and went immediately into the TV business. For the next two decades, I produced screen content but rarely watched it.

Then in 2003, my screen addiction came calling in the form of a PowerBook G4 laptop computer with broadband internet and a wireless router. The combination of portability, Wi-Fi, and the World Wide Web proved irresistible. I carried that laptop to my easy chair in the evening and into my bedroom at night. Unlike my father, whose TV brought in fewer than a dozen channels, my computer provided an inexhaustible supply of entertainment, websites, email messages, and news updates. As a result, my screen time began to rival my father's.

By the late 2000s, more and more of my attention was absorbed by that little thirteen-inch LCD panel. In the process, I was slowly losing touch with the real world. My body was home, but my mind was in cyberspace. I didn't notice my absence, but my wife and kids did. One autumn day, they confronted me about my obsession with screen time. I faced the truth: I was trading away real life for screen life, just as my father had.

I wish I could say I declared victory that day, but each new screen technology has brought with it unexpected temptations.

About three years ago, a buddy invited me to try Words with Friends. It's like Scrabble, but you play it on your phone. It was an entertaining way to pass the time whenever I had a few minutes to kill: standing in line at the grocery store, waiting at the baggage carousel, or sitting alone in my easy chair. I reckoned I was playing about an hour or two a week, so it was no big deal. I was still getting my work done and spending time with my loved ones.

Then Apple introduced iOS 12, which automatically issues a weekly screen-time summary. When I saw my first report, I dropped to my knees. Over the previous seven days I had blown more than *twelve hours* playing Words with Friends. Once again, the hypnotic power of a glowing screen had blinded me to my obsession. I was angry at myself for wasting so much time in pursuit of something so meaningless.

I immediately deleted the game. Those first few days were difficult. I instinctively reached for my phone dozens of times. I felt as though I was disappointing my friends for dropping out of matches already in progress. But over time, my desire to play faded. And what did I do with those extra twelve hours a week? I began researching the book you hold in your hand.

So let's dive in. I'm going to start you off with a series of easy-to-remember tales, which I'm calling the Five Parables. I'll have one more for you later in the book.

A parable is a big truth wrapped in a little story. The entire book is built atop these parables, so don't skip over them. Only then will the rest of this book make sense.

SECTION I

The Five Parables

1.1

The Parable of Max and the Sea

After weeks of walking, Max reached Land's End. Before him lay a sapphire ocean. Frothy waves expired on the beach as seagulls cried overhead.

Max had never seen such a wonder. As a man of the high country, the only bodies of water he knew were rivers, lakes, and ponds. Waves had always meant a gathering storm.

But the day was fair—hot, in fact—so Max removed his outer garments, kicked off his shoes, and stepped into the sea. Cooling wavelets met his toes, and sand began massaging the soles of his aching feet.

Max waded in up to his ankles. He felt no danger, only pleasure as gentle swells lapped at his tired calves. He stepped further into the soothing waters—knee-deep, hip-deep, and then waist-deep. He began to feel buoyant as seawater cradled his lower body.

Max hardly noticed as the undertow began carrying him farther out until he was chest-deep and eventually neck-deep. He felt a mixture of fright and exhilaration as large waves lifted him off his feet and crashed over his head. Max felt no alarm; he could see the shoreline at a distance and touch the seafloor below.

Max noticed a bulbous, white creature floating near the surface of the water. Then another and another. They were all around him. As he reached out to touch one, he felt a sharp twinge of pain just above his left ankle. Then something stung his lower back. Max detected the faint outline of tentacles descending like vines from the creatures' watery bodies. He tried to wade back to shore but struggled to gain his footing in the deep, churning waters. He was stung again and again. Max began to feel lightheaded and disoriented.

Then came a rogue wave that knocked him backward. He gasped for breath as his body tumbled violently. He tried to stand, but the seafloor was gone. He briefly spotted the shoreline and attempted to paddle back, but waves kept pounding him, and a rip current carried him farther out to sea.

The same waters that had welcomed Max so pleasurably now ushered him to his grave.

The Parable of Max and the Sea Explained

In this parable, Max represents humanity. The land (both the shore and seafloor) represents real life. The water represents screen life.

Just as Max had never seen an ocean, humanity had never seen a screen until December 28, 1895, when the Lumiére brothers unveiled the world's first film-projection system in a Paris café. For the next fifty years, screens existed only in movie theaters. People typically saw one motion picture a month, placing them ankle-deep in screen time.

Screens began showing up in our homes in the late 1940s with the advent of broadcast television. By 1960, 85 percent of American homes had a TV set, and screen time became an everyday pleasure. Humanity was then knee-deep in screen time.

Beginning in the 1970s, a host of new technologies pulled us deeper into the screen world. Home video cassette recorders (VCRs) and an explosion of new cable networks increased our enjoyment, raising screen time to waist-level. Video games and personal computers made our screens interactive, pushing the water up to our chests. Then came wireless computing and smartphones, making screen time an anytime, anywhere experience. By the 2010s, we were up to our necks in screen time, devoting the vast majority of our spare attention to our glowing companions. We experienced a mixture of fright and exhilaration as our screens lifted us to new heights of productivity and diversion. Few of us sensed any danger. We could still see the shore and the seafloor (real life).

Max felt curiosity as he saw his first jellyfish bobbing peacefully atop the waves. It looked so harmless. In the same way, many of us have followed our curiosity to some unhealthy screen activities. "I can handle this," we tell ourselves as our souls are poisoned one little sting at a time. Our physical, mental, and spiritual health deteriorate. We become disoriented and lose sight of real life.

The rogue wave represents the COVID-19 pandemic that washed over the planet in 2020. Nobody saw it coming. The lockdowns suddenly plunged everyone into the deep waters of screen time. Friends gathered on screen, coworkers collaborated on screen, and students attended classes on screen. Many churches offered on-screen worship services for the first time. We were thankful that screens kept us in touch in a time of social distancing.

But the sudden immersion in screen life will cause many more of us to drown. In the first weeks of the lockdowns, web traffic increased 20 percent. Video streaming rose 12 percent, and online gaming spiked 75 percent.[1] The world's largest porn site saw an 18 percent increase in visits.[2] America's leading pharmacy plan manager dispensed 34 percent more anti-anxiety pills and 19 percent more anti-depressants.[3] Alcohol sales spiked 55 percent during the first week of the lockdowns,[4] and the United Nations reported a "horrifying surge" in domestic violence worldwide.[5] Reports of online child abuse increased fourfold, as predators targeted youngsters who were spending more time on screens.[6] One wonders if these trends are the new normal.

If Max had encountered the jellyfish and the rogue wave in shallower waters, he would easily have survived. Beach swimming isn't particularly hazardous if you stay close to the shore. The enemy is the undertow, which constantly pulls the swimmer out to sea.

In the same way, screen time isn't particularly hazardous when used by adults in moderation and for noble purposes. But screens exert a powerful pull on our time and attention, dragging us deeper into their world without our realizing it.

■   ■   ■

Here's the lesson of the first parable: screen time often carries us into deep, treacherous waters.

The Parable of the Fishbowl

Sam likes to play table tennis, better known as ping-pong. He keeps his ping-pong balls in a glass fishbowl.

Over the years, he's added more and more balls to his fishbowl, and it's become quite full.

But it's not completely full. There's still a lot of empty space between the balls.

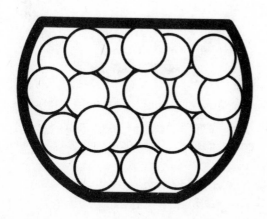

One day, Sam notices that the balls are looking scuffed and dirty. So he fills a pitcher with water and pours it into the fishbowl.

Two things happen:

1. All the empty spaces between the balls are filled with water.
2. Balls begin rising to the top and spilling out of the fishbowl.

But Sam keeps adding water because the balls need a good cleaning.

The Parable of the Fishbowl Explained

The fishbowl represents your brain's total capacity. And each ping-pong ball represents something we do or think about.

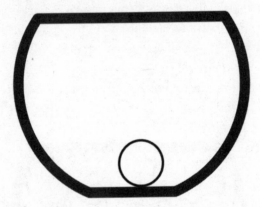

Every worry, dream, thought, goal, and emotion is a ping-pong ball. So are relationships, work, school, leisure activities, responsibilities, sleeping, eating, and socializing. Each one is represented by a ball.

Over the centuries, the number of balls in our brains has increased. People have more to think about than ever before because we have more choices than ever. And all these options have filled our fishbowls to capacity.

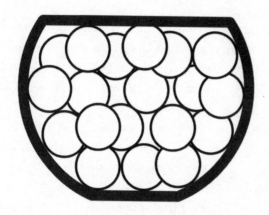

My fishbowl is quite full. Yours probably is too.

Here are just a few of my ping-pong balls: *Family. Finances. Hobbies. Scheduling. Volunteering. Career. Dreams for the future. Regrets from the past. Friends. Health. Entertainment. That person I'd like to meet for coffee. That car repair I need to get done. Getting this book written and off to the publisher.* Most days my to-do list is overflowing. My brain has a lot of things to do and think about.

But even the fullest brain (and schedule) has little moments of downtime between activities. Those moments are represented by the small pockets of airspace between the balls.

This precious downtime is crucial to our physical, mental, and spiritual health. Our brains literally rest and repair themselves during these intervals of non-activity—preparing us for the next challenge we'll face.

Now, back to ping-pong-playing Sam. When he filled the fishbowl with water, what happened to that airspace between the balls? It was displaced, and balls started popping out the top.

In this parable, the water represents screen time. It's filling every spare moment of our attention. Drowning out creativity. Pushing out thinking time. Displacing spiritual disciplines such as prayer and meditation. Keeping us focused on the trivial rather than the important.

Are you doubtful? What's the first thing we do in the morning? Check our phones. Over breakfast we watch a little morning TV or spend a few minutes on social media. Subway riders hardly look up from their devices. Lunch break? We're on our phones. Got a minute standing in line at the bank or grocery store? We whip out our phones. As soon as we're home, we turn on the TV and grab our laptops. Finally, we brush our teeth and slip into bed, tablets in hand. Our phones watch over us as we sleep, serving as our alarm clocks, never leaving our sides.

Tell me, when do our brains rest? Only when we sleep. We fill every spare waking moment with screen time. And it's come to this: three-quarters of Americans admit to using their phones in the bathroom.[1] Even toilet time has become screen time.

Marathon runners know the importance of having rest days to let their bodies recover between training runs. But our brains are running marathons every hour of every day with hardly a breather.

It's ironic: Our fishbowls are full. We feel stressed. So we turn to our screens for relief. Instead of giving our brains the downtime they need, we further stimulate them, which feels good in the moment. But the additional screen time drowns out what little mental capacity remains, increasing our tension and anxiety.

The water not only fills all the empty spaces between ping-pong balls; it also pushes some balls out of the bowl altogether. Screen time is displacing things that are vitally important, leaving us with less time and energy to invest in the people and activities that make life worth living.

Screens trick our subconscious minds into thinking we're doing great things. Video games make us feel heroic and powerful. Romantic movies give us the feeling of being loved and cherished. Social media fools us into believing we are living in community.

But these things aren't real. They're synthetic, computer-generated substitutes. Our next parable will explain why humans so happily trade real life for an illusion.

■   ■   ■

Here is the lesson of the second parable: screen time leaves us drowning in distraction.

1.3

The Parable of the Matrix

The world is not what you think it is.

I've recently discovered the truth. Everything we see, feel, hear, smell, and taste is just a computer-generated simulation.

Artificial intelligence has enslaved humanity for its own cruel purposes. The system is able to control us by projecting a computer-generated illusion into each individual's brain. We imagine ourselves to be free, but in reality our bodies are captive to a giant machine.

The machine is called the Matrix.

The Parable of the Matrix Explained

On April 2, 1999, I took my eleven-year-old son to see his first R-rated film: *The Matrix*.

The Matrix is one of the most innovative movies ever produced. It won four Academy Awards. As I write this, it is the sixteenth most popular film of all time among the thousands listed on Internet Movie Database (IMDb).

The film is set two hundred years in the future. Artificial intelligence has enslaved humanity, but humanity doesn't realize it. That's because the Matrix is able to project a computer-generated fantasy directly into the brains of its captives. People think they are free, but in reality their bodies are being exploited by a massive machine.

The film revolves around a character named Neo, a computer hacker who begins to realize things are not as they seem. He is contacted by Morpheus, a mysterious character who has freed himself from the Matrix. At their first meeting, Morpheus offers Neo two pills: one red, the other blue. If Neo swallows the blue pill, he'll remain in the Matrix, living out his life in peaceful deception. If he takes the red pill, his eyes will open, and he'll see the world as it is—freed from the machine. Morpheus warns Neo that the real world is a ghastly place. But Neo doesn't hesitate. He swallows the red pill and begins to learn the truth.

Eventually, Morpheus shows Neo the real world (on a TV screen, ironically). It's a post-apocalyptic hellscape of burned-out buildings and desolate emptiness under a blackened sky. Neo is so shaken that he asks Morpheus if it's possible to abandon this dreadful reality and return to the Matrix.

And if you want to know the rest of the story, you'll have to watch the movie.

Now, back to real life. After we left the theater, my son turned to me and said, "Dad, that was a good movie, but I have a question. How would the computers trick people into going into the Matrix in the first place?"

"Well, you saw how bad the real world was," I answered. "All they would have to do is convince people that a digital simulation was better than real life. Soon they would forget the real world and come to believe in the Matrix."

And that's exactly what's happening today. Billions of people around the world are choosing screen-based fantasy over real life. Why? Our screens are convincing us that our lives are horrible and the world is on the verge of collapse, even though we actually live in the most peaceful, prosperous time in history.

Why would the producers of screen content do this to us? Because bad news gets our attention. Good news doesn't. And once media companies have our attention, it can be sold to advertisers for big money.

This is why every media conglomerate has two divisions: a news side and an entertainment side. The news division serves up an endless stream of conflict, controversy, and crisis. Once you're frightened and upset, the news division hands you over to the entertainment division to be soothed by a TV show, sporting event, or movie. Along the way, both divisions sell your attention to advertisers.

So is the Matrix real? Is there a malevolent computer controlling your smartphone, trying to enslave you? No. Artificial Intelligence isn't running the world—yet. However, the trends are clear: every year people retreat a little more from real life and spend a few more minutes in the Matrix.

■   ■   ■

Here is the lesson of the third parable: screen time leaves us drowning in illusion.

1.4

The Parable of David and the Wolf

Meet David, a shepherd boy living about three thousand years ago in the Middle East.

Every day, David leads his flocks into green pastures and beside still waters. David watches the sun rise. He watches the sun set. He counts sheep by day and stars by night. His world consists of grass, rocks, trees, water, dung, flies, and—of course—sheep.

David's life is one of monotony. Day after day and night after night, nothing much happens. He plays his harp to pass the time. He composes psalms in his head. He practices his slingshot.

Then one lazy afternoon, David hears a sheep cry out. He bolts upright. A lone wolf has a lamb in its jaws.

David quickly calculates the distance between himself, the wolf, and the trees. The predator is seconds away from the cover of forest. The lamb's only hope of rescue is David's trusty slingshot. He reaches into his pouch, loads a stone, and lets it fly.

ZING!

The missile finds its target. The wolf cries out in pain, drops its prey, and runs into the woods.

David rushes to the frightened lamb and takes it into his arms. *Victory!*

Fortunately, the predator does not return. Things return to normal, peaceful monotony.

David continues to spend his idle hours practicing his slingshot, because you never know when you're going to face another wolf—or perhaps a giant.

The Parable of David and the Wolf Explained

For almost all of human history, life has consisted of long periods of monotony followed by rare moments of novelty.

Monotony has always been life's normal state. Almost all people who have ever lived have spent their entire lives among their kin, rarely traveling more than a few miles from home. They did the same jobs, ate the same foods, and wore the same attire day after day after day.

Our brains are designed for this monotonous world. They expect routine and lots of it.

But every once in a while, something unusual happens to break the monotony. We call this *novelty*.

Novelty is abnormal. It has always meant danger or opportunity. Something you could eat—or something that could eat you. That's why our brains contain an advanced surveillance/alarm system that is triggered in response to anything out of the ordinary.

When David spotted the wolf among his flock, his brain and body went into a state known as hyperarousal (commonly known as adrenaline rush or fight-or-flight mode). Within seconds, hormones flooded his brain. His heart rate, blood pressure, and respiration increased. David's pupils dilated, and his peripheral vision decreased to better focus on the threat. His blood sugar ramped up for quick energy.

Even after he rescued the lamb, David's internal systems remained stimulated for almost an hour. His brain's reward circuitry was awash in dopamine, a neurotransmitter that produces a shot of pleasure.

Fast-forward to today. Those regions of our brain that were designed to respond to occasional novelty are being overstimulated. Instead of firing every few days, they are firing every few seconds. That novelty is provided by our screens. Televisions. Computers. Video games. And especially smartphones.

No longer do we live in a world of monotony, waiting for something new to see. Visual novelty is available to us every waking moment. We carry an unlimited supply of visual novelty with us everywhere we go. The wolf appears often. And we can summon him anytime we want.

Let me emphasize this again: Access to constant novelty is completely unnatural. Our brains have never experienced anything like it. And each time we see something new, we are rewarded with a squirt of the feel-good chemical dopamine. Dr. Nicholas Kardaras explains how this works:

> The most primitive parts of our brain—the medulla and cerebellum—cradle our ancient dopamine-reward pathways. And when an action has a feel-good result—like finding food or discovering something new on the Internet or in a video game—dopamine is released, which feels

pleasurable and creates a more-we-get-more-we-want addictive cycle.

Unlike our ancestors, who were in fight-or-flight adrenal arousal for only brief, acute periods of emergency—like being chased by a lion—today's tech keeps the adrenaline and fight-or-flight response on perpetual high alert for hour after hour....[1]

I am not suggesting that a TV show, website, or video game arouses our brains with the same intensity as a predator attack. However, screen content stimulates the same regions of the brain. Dr. Victoria Dunckley writes:

Interacting with screens shifts the nervous system into fight-or-flight mode which leads to dysregulation and disorganization of various biological systems. Sometimes this stress response is immediate and pronounced (say while playing an action video game), and other times the response is more subtle and may happen only after a certain amount of repetition (say while texting).... In short, though, interacting with screen devices causes a child to become overstimulated and "revved up."[2]

It's not just children who experience this overstimulation. The more we adults look at screens, the more our brains experience a mild version of "fight or flight." The effect is subtle in the moment, but over time it quietly rewires our brains, training them to seek constant stimulation. Neuroscientist Daniel J. Levitin writes:

Each time we dispatch an email in one way or another, we feel a sense of accomplishment, and our brain gets a dollop of reward hormones telling us we accomplished something.

Each time we check a Twitter feed or Facebook update, we encounter something novel and feel more connected socially (in a kind of weird, impersonal cyber way) and get another dollop of reward hormones.... Make no mistake: email-, Facebook- and Twitter-checking constitute a neural addiction.[3]

This is why we instantly pick up our phones the moment we're bored. There's no burning need to see what's happened on Instagram in the seven minutes since we last checked. Our subconscious brains are in charge, calling for a droplet of dopamine, and our bodies mindlessly comply.

Meanwhile, we push aside activities that require long concentration. Reading a novel, completing a project, or tending a relationship do not give our brains the incessant novelty they crave. Instead, we scurry from screen to screen like rats in search of cheese, looking for a dopamine hit that will relieve our stress and give us a moment of mild pleasure.

Need proof? Go to any airport, shopping mall, or public park. What are people doing? Independent, creative thinking? Relating to one another? Daydreaming? No—they're buried in their phones, stimulating their brains by summoning the wolf.

■   ■   ■

Here is the lesson of the fourth parable: screen time leaves us drowning in novelty.

1.5

The Parable of the Kingdom

Remember David the shepherd boy from our last parable? Well, you'll never guess what happened: the runt son of a common animal herder grew up to become king.

As a poor shepherd, David's life was mundane. But as the king of Israel, he moved from a tent into a fortified palace. Inside those walls, his life changed forever.

The newly crowned king instantly gained access to a vast array of treasures, pleasures, and diversions unavailable to the common man. The world's riches were suddenly within his grasp. Any food he desired could appear on his table each night. With a clap of his hands, David could summon musicians, dancers, and entertainers to perform for his amusement. When the evening's festivities were over, the king retired to his bedchamber, where a harem of beautiful women waited to fulfill his every desire.

King David no longer obeyed decrees; he issued them. His mandates were posted in the public square and read by heralds throughout the land. As king, his judgments and opinions were by definition the correct ones—to be obeyed without question.

The king assembled wise men to guide him on matters of state. Theirs was a difficult task, since the king didn't like being contradicted. Over time, his cabinet filled with "Yes-Men" who affirmed his positions and praised his acumen.

Information is power, and David regularly dispatched spies and messengers to gather intelligence. As a result, he was always alert to potential threats. The king carried the burden of this knowledge every day of his reign.

David maintained power by vanquishing foes. He put heretics, turncoats, and rivals to the sword. He banished enemies and publicly humiliated adversaries.

King David understood the importance of popularity and worked tirelessly to project an image of strength to the populace.

Over time, he became disconnected from his former life: his father, his brothers, and the common people who populated his kingdom. It's lonely at the top, and David experienced the isolation that accompanies power. A monarch can never quite drop his guard. He must watch his words and remain suspicious of everyone he meets. Betrayers lurk around every corner.

In the end, the responsibilities of maintaining a kingdom became too much. He sequestered himself in his palace, sending his men off to war while he feasted and slept. The bored king took another man's wife into his bed, got her pregnant, and then had her husband murdered to cover up the scandal.

From that day forward, rebellion, rape, and death engulfed his house. The king descended into a deep depression, desperately clinging to power, even as his sons rose up against him. In those dark days, David looked back longingly to the simple shepherd's life he once enjoyed. He poured his anxieties into poetry and songs, many of which survive to this day.

The Parable of the Kingdom Explained

Of all the pernicious effects screens are having on us, perhaps none is as harmful as this:

Screens encourage us to build personal digital kingdoms. Within these virtual castle walls, we reign as lords and masters. We exercise absolute control over what we see, what we play, who comes in, and which ideas will be tolerated. We spend an average of nine hours a day in this artificial realm. Over time, we become accustomed to living in a world that bends to our will.

Then we go back into the real world, where almost nothing bends to our will. Real life has no on/off button. There's no way to "unfriend" toxic co-workers, nor can we change the channel when our car breaks down. There's no guarantee of a happy ending when an injustice is done, a relationship goes sour, or illness strikes.

Psychologists are seeing an unprecedented spike in depression and anxiety, especially among young people who have grown up online. Critics dismiss them as "snowflakes," but their fragility is a byproduct of having been raised in a digital world they can customize and manipulate. When the real world does not yield to their preferences, they experience angst. Having spent so much time immersed in screen life, they find themselves poorly equipped to deal with the challenges of real life.

Like the kings and queens of old, digital lords and ladies are becoming paralyzed by choice, overwhelmed by Fear of Missing Out (FOMO), targeted by hucksters and extremists, and isolated from reality. Consider the parallels between David and our modern-day digital kings and queens:

The Newly Crowned King Gained Access to a Vast Array of Treasures, Pleasures, and Diversions

History's wealthiest monarch never could have imagined the vast marketplace of goods and services our screens place in front of us. As of 2019, e-commerce giant Amazon.com offered more than 119 million products that are available to anyone with a smartphone and a credit card.[1] Click "buy now" and the world's treasures are rushed to our doors with free next-day shipping.

And Amazon is just one site. The internet is home to hundreds of thousands of online marketplaces offering millions of goods and services. This vast marketplace is open 24/7 and can be accessed from almost any place on Earth. King David would have been stupefied. But there's more...

When David clapped his hands, sumptuous food appeared on his table. We can achieve the same via our phones. Urban dwellers can now order any cuisine imaginable—from Afghani to Zanzibari—and have it delivered. Feel like cooking? Tap on your screen and groceries appear within hours.

Kings relied on troupes of local entertainers. But today's digital royals can summon any musician, actor, or comedian they want, any time of the day or night, at virtually no cost, thanks to streaming video and audio. We can even rouse the dead to sing, dance, and act for us. Johnny Cash passed away in 2003, but the Man in Black sang for me as I cleaned out my garage last night.

Ancient potentates enjoyed the pleasures of a harem—a collection of wives and concubines received as peace offerings from rival kings. But today's digital royals can gaze upon an endless selection of the world's most beautiful people. TV shows and movies present the viewer with a ceaseless procession of stunning faces and perfectly toned bodies. Log into a dating app and thousands of potential romantic partners appear instantly. But why bother dating a real person? Online pornography gives digital monarchs access to a virtual harem of simulated sex partners who are always willing and available.

King David No Longer Obeyed Decrees; He Issued Them

In ancient times, only kings and popes had the power to issue a decree and have it read throughout the realm. But today, with the advent of social media and blogs, anyone with a smartphone and pair of thumbs can express an opinion and post it for the world to see.

This has led to an outbreak of dogmatism online. Armed with kingly confidence, digital royals pronounce judgment with absolute certainty, denigrating anyone whose opinions diverge even slightly from their own. The attitude is this: *I'm absolutely right. Those who disagree with me must be confused, stupid, or evil.*

Why is the current generation of college students so quick to censor free speech? Because they've been deleting posts they disagree with on social media since they were thirteen years old. Social media taught them to shout down and shut out people and opinions they find unacceptable.

All this screen-inspired hubris has led to an online "narcissism epidemic" among young adults.[2] Meanwhile, civility, humility, and empathy seem to be on the decline in both the screen world and the real world.

Algorithms—the Web's Yes-Men

Like the courtiers of old, algorithms are the digital equivalent of Yes-Men. They look over our shoulders as we surf the web and then push content our way that confirms what we already believe. Algorithms make it hard for any dissenting views to breach the walls of our digital castles. I'll explain how algorithms both coddle and divide us in Chapter 2.9.

Information Is Power, and Kings Stay in the Know

Never has the most powerful sultan, sage, or scholar had instant access to the vast library of information we carry in our pockets. Want to know Wednesday's weather forecast? Need directions to the nearest pharmacy? A video review of a vehicle you're thinking of buying? The origin of the word *cummerbund* (yes, that's how it's spelled—there's only one B). Digital royals have access to almost any fact they could want within seconds.

Of course, information is not wisdom. There's a lot of misinformation on the web, and it's leading to an outbreak of conspiracy theories and hoaxes. Algorithms make things worse by confirming our biases and stoking our fears. Relationships erode as we turn to the Web instead of each other for counsel.

David Maintained Power by Eliminating Foes and Leading His Country into War

Young David had to learn to live with difficult people. As an impoverished shepherd boy, he was stuck with his tribe, including seven older brothers who probably used him as a punching bag. But as monarch, David controlled who came into his royal presence, as can we. Digital royals can exile annoying people from social media by unfriending or banning them. *Poof*, they're gone, never to bother us again.

David put heretics, turncoats, and rivals to death, and we can do the same thing online. Doxing, cyber-shaming, and attacks from Twitter mobs have cost people scholarships, awards, and careers. The offense can be something as minor as a foolish tweet or an ill-advised photo from decades ago. Meanwhile, pre-pubescent teens are literally killing one another via cyberbullying.[3]

Kings have always led troops into war. And thanks to video games, we too can command a simulated army. Our brains experience the thrill of combat while our bodies sit on the couch, munching Doritos.

As King, David Worked Tirelessly to Maintain an Image of Strength among the Populace

David came to power based on his reputation as a giant killer, and he knew how important it was to project an image of strength and invulnerability. Social media encourages us to do the same. It's called "image crafting." Here's a simple definition: using social media to present a perfect life to your friends, family, and fans.

Most of us image craft without even realizing it. We happily post the good things about our lives: vacations, weddings, graduations, and, of course, plated dinners. But we omit anything that might show us in a negative light.

#blessed

David Became More and More Isolated

David's life went off the rails when he sequestered himself inside his royal palace. Screens encourage us to do the same.

As we spend the bulk of our free time in our digital castles, we're becoming lonelier than ever. Like King David, we are losing touch with real life. Depression and suicide rates among the young spiked at exactly the same time that smartphones were introduced. Unlimited choice is bringing with it unprecedented anxiety.

■   ■   ■

Here is the meaning of the fifth parable: screen time leaves us drowning in choice.

1.6

A Recap of the Five Parables

shared these parables to give us a common set of metaphors as we
discuss screen use, overuse, and abuse. I'll be referring to them
repeatedly throughout the rest of the book. To make sure you've got
them down, here's a quick recap of the parables and their meanings:

1. **Max and the Sea:** Screen time often carries us into deep,
   treacherous waters. The wise screen user stays close to
   shore (real life) and avoids jellyfish (unhealthy content
   and activities).
2. **The Fishbowl:** Screen time leaves us drowning in distraction, filling every spare moment of our time and
   attention, denying our brains time to recover and rest,
   and displacing more important things.
3. **The Matrix:** Screen time leaves us drowning in illusion.
   News media outlets raise our anxiety and then hand us
   off to the entertainment media to be soothed.

4. **David and the Wolf:** Screen content leaves us drowning in novelty, keeping our nervous systems in a hyper-stimulated "fight-or-flight" mode for extended periods of time.

5. **The Kingdom:** Screen content leaves us drowning in choice. Within our digital kingdoms, we experience powers, privileges, and pressures that were once reserved for royalty. Overwhelmed by options, we tend to hide in our castles, which leads to loneliness and anxiety.

Now you're ready for the rest of the book.

I Want to Understand the Effects of Screen Use, Both Good and Bad

2.1

Nine Hours a Day. Really?

During the 1940s, televisions began showing up in the display windows of electronics stores across America. Huge crowds gathered on sidewalks to watch tiny black-and-white images of entertainers, athletes, and politicians captured by cameras far away and sent over the airwaves in real time. People marveled. You could stand on a street corner in Chicago and see a baseball being thrown in Yankee Stadium eight hundred miles away.

Today, such a display would not merit a second glance. Screens are everywhere. One can hardly walk through an airport, dine at a restaurant, or attend a church service without encountering these glimmering monoliths. In less than a century, screens went from being an unprecedented novelty to our ever-present companions. According to a 2019 report from Pew Research Center:

> Mobile technology has spread rapidly around the globe.
> Today, it is estimated that more than five billion people

have mobile devices, and over half of these connections are smartphones [the rest are traditional mobile phones with buttons].[1]

It's hard to grasp the degree to which screens have come to dominate our attention in such a short time. But let's try. I'm going to hit you with a lot of facts and figures in this chapter. If numbers aren't your thing, then let me sum up what they are telling us: Just one generation ago, adults and children spent the majority of their leisure time in the real world. Today, they spend the bulk of it in the screen world.

Adults' Average Screen Time: Nine Hours a Day and Rising

A 2018 report from Nielsen Media Research found that the average American adult spends eleven hours a day interacting with media—not counting the time they use screens at work.[2] Almost two of those hours are devoted to listening (to the radio or streaming music). That leaves just over nine hours of screen time each day. Keep in mind that this is an average, so many people spend even more time glued to their screens.

Traditional TV (cable, satellite, and over-the-air) is still king. But wireless interactive media (which includes the computer, tablet, and smartphone added together) is catching up quickly. High-speed wireless connectivity barely existed at the turn of the twenty-first century, and now portable devices that access the internet capture our attention an average of three hours and forty-eight minutes a day.

Another survey from eMarketer found that the average American spends an incredible ten hours a day interacting with screen media.[3] You may ask, "How is this possible?" Multitasking—like watching TV while scrolling through social media:

Six of those daily hours are spent on our smartphones, tablets, or laptops. During our daily media smorgasbord, we are seeing between 4,000-10,000 ads per day. In about the minute it will take you to read this paragraph, in the US alone another seven million videos will be watched on Snapchat; Instagram users will like over two-and-a-half million posts; and three-and-a-half million text messages will be sent.[4]

The U.S. Bureau of Labor Statistics tracks how Americans spend their time and publishes its findings in the American Time Use Survey (ATUS). According to ATUS, in 2018, the average American aged fifteen or older spent 5.27 hours a day in leisure and sports activities and devoted more than half of those hours to watching TV.[5]

Although ATUS identified fewer hours of daily media use than the Nielsen survey cited above, both studies agree on this: Americans' leisure time is dominated by screens, particularly TV. Good old-fashioned cable and over-the-air television gobble up anywhere from half to two-thirds of our free hours every day. Seniors watch the most TV (hence the large number of advertisements for hearing aids and prescription drugs on traditional television), but even teens and young adults sink about 40 percent of their free time into the TV. Among all age groups, watching television consumes just over half of all leisure time:

Why do we still watch so much TV? Because it's the easiest, fastest way to run up the drawbridge and hide in our digital castles. TV is easy. Just press the power button and it's there. TV makes no demands; it merely entertains.

A lot of you are probably shaking your heads. *TV? Really?* Really. That's why I didn't title this book *Drowning in Your Smartphone.* TV is still America's go-to screen activity. Why do you think Costco parks those gigantic televisions right by the front door of its warehouses?

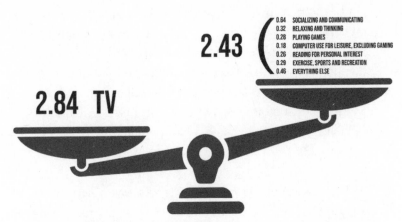

0.64 SOCIALIZING AND COMMUNICATING
0.32 RELAXING AND THINKING
0.28 PLAYING GAMES
0.18 COMPUTER USE FOR LEISURE, EXCLUDING GAMING
0.26 READING FOR PERSONAL INTEREST
0.29 EXERCISE, SPORTS AND RECREATION
0.46 EVERYTHING ELSE

2.43

2.84 TV

2018 – HOURS SPENT IN EACH ACTIVITY PER DAY, AMERICANS AGE 15 +

PERCENTAGE OF LEISURE TIME SPENT WATCHING BROADCAST OR CABLE TV, BY AGE GROUP

Age Group	Hours per day	Percentage of leisure time watching TV
Total, age 15+	2.84	54 percent
15 to 24-year-olds	2.12	39 percent
25 to 34-year-olds	2.03	48 percent
35 to 44-year-olds	2.12	52 percent
45 to 54-year-olds	2.56	56 percent
55 to 64-year-olds	3.36	61 percent
65+	4.52	61 percent

Source: U.S. Bureau of Labor Statistics[6]

You would expect adults to cut back on watching TV after they discovered new screen entertainment options, but for the most part, that hasn't been the case. Although watching TV is down a little (especially among the young), we just keep layering new forms of screen time on top of our existing television habit. Americans frequently watch TV and scroll their mobile devices simultaneously, filling their fishbowls twice as quickly.

Adults use screens a lot—but how about teens? If adults are this obsessed with screens, aren't teens even worse?

The answer is a qualified yes. Although young people spend fewer total hours per day on their screens than adults, the gap is narrowing rapidly.

Common Sense Media studied screen use among eight- to eighteen-year-olds across the U.S. in 2015 and 2019 to identify trends, many of which illustrate how rapidly screens are taking over the lives of young people.[7]

Common Sense Media CEO James P. Steyer writes:

> [Y]oung people are spending significant time on screens every day, with 8- to 12-year-olds now on them for an average of about five hours a day, and teens clocking about seven and a half hours of screen time daily—not including at school or for homework. Their habits mirror the new media trends. Television watching is down, and online video viewing is through the roof: More than twice as many young people watch videos every day than did in 2015, and the average daily time spent watching, mostly YouTube, has roughly doubled to an hour each day. Watching online videos is the most popular activity among tweens and ranks second only to listening to music among teens.
>
> The jump in media use is also impacting other parts of young people's lives. We know from previous research that a majority of teens sleep with their phones within reach, disrupting vital rest. This census shows that nearly a third of teens in this country say they read for pleasure less than once a month, if at all. And access to tech continues to age

down, with the number of 8-year-olds with phones growing from 11 percent in 2015 to 19 percent today.

Here are some of the group's detailed findings:

1. Traditional TV-watching is falling among younger viewers. Both tweens and teens watch about a half hour less of broadcast or cable TV (just twenty-five minutes a day in 2019, down from fifty-four minutes in 2015). Instead, they are watching more time-shifted TV (DVR) or streamed programming from subscription platforms such as Amazon Prime.

2. Teens and tweens are ditching traditional TV shows in favor of videos. Some are professionally produced long-form programs, but many more are short, amateur productions posted on video-sharing apps. The percentage of young people who say they watch online videos every day more than doubled between 2015 and 2019, and the amount of time each age group spends watching online videos has doubled from about a half hour a day to an hour a day on average (from twenty-five to fifty-six minutes a day among tweens and from thirty-five to fifty-nine minutes a day among teens). Watching online videos is more popular than social media or gaming.

3. Among tweens, about half (53 percent) of all screen time is devoted to watching TV or videos and 31 percent to gaming. Websites and social media absorb just 5 percent and 4 percent of tweens' screen time, with video chatting (2 percent), e-reading (2 percent), or creating content (such as writing or making digital art or music) at 2 percent.

4. Among teens, 39 percent of screen use is devoted to watching TV or videos, 22 percent to gaming, and 16

percent to social media. Four percent is spent video chatting, 3 percent creating their own writing, art, or music, and 2 percent e-reading.

5. Tweens and teens who live in lower-income households spend about 1.75 more hours a day on their screens than their higher-income peers. The average low-income teen spends a staggering 8.5 hours a day interacting with screen entertainment.

6. Social media is most popular among Hispanic teens, who devote two hours and twenty-three minutes a day to it; white teens spend one hour and thirty-five minutes on it. The number of teens who say they use social media every day increased from 45 percent in 2015 to 63 percent in 2019.

7. Experts tout the creative potential of screens, but not many young people are using them to produce original content. Fewer than one in ten tweens or teens create digital art or graphics, music, videos, websites, or games.

8. In 2019, twice as many tweens and teens used computers and tablets for homework every day as did in 2015.

9. Boys and girls have vastly different tastes in media. Seventy percent of boys say they enjoy playing video games a lot, compared to just 23 percent of girls. Forty-one percent of boys play games every day, compared to just 9 percent of girls. On the flip side, 50 percent of girls enjoy social media a lot, compared to 32 percent of boys. Teen girls devote ninety minutes a day to social media, while their male counterparts average just fifty-one minutes a day.

10. And I saved the worst for last: By age eleven, 53 percent of American kids have their own smartphone. By age twelve, 69 percent do. These numbers have risen

dramatically since 2015. A solid majority of American sixth graders now carry the internet in their pockets.

Conclusion: Tween and teen screen use is exploding. Look for those numbers to climb even higher in the years to come.

But what about the youngest children—those under eight? Surely parents are not putting the internet in those little hands. Or are they?

Common Sense Media reported on trends among children from birth to eight years old in 2011, 2013, and 2017: [8]

1. Just 1 percent of kids eight or under had their own tablets in 2011. By 2017, that figure was 42 percent and rising.
2. In 2011, young children spent an average of just five minutes a day on mobile devices. By 2013, that tripled to fifteen minutes. And by 2017, it tripled again to forty-eight minutes per day.
3. Children ages five to eight spend more time on video game consoles, computers, and mobile devices than they do watching TV (broadcast, cable, streamed, and DVD combined).
4. Nearly half of kids in this age group are on screens in the hour before bedtime.
5. Forty-two percent of parents say the TV is on in the house "always or most of the time."
6. Children from lower-income homes spend an average of 3.5 hours a day with screen media, compared to 1.8 hours a day in higher-income homes.
7. Less-educated parents allow their kids to use screens an hour and thirteen minutes longer per day than their more highly educated peers.

8. Parents are concerned about what their offspring see on the screen: three-quarters worry about exposing their kids to violent and sexual content. Sixty-nine percent worry about advertising and materialism.
9. Seventy percent of parents are somewhat or very concerned about the amount of time their young children spend on screens.

Here's what rings alarm bells for me: Almost half of kids under the age of eight have their own tablets. Instead of encouraging our youngest children to get into the real world and occupy themselves by developing their imaginations, we are training them to turn to their screens the moment they're bored. By six years old, these tots are already becoming tiny lords of their personal digital realms, accustomed to living in an artificial world that offers them constant stimulation and entertainment. Let's hope these tablets aren't connected to the World Wide Web. Is your average six-year-old ready for that?

■   ■   ■

Whether the precise number of hours we spend looking at our screens each day is five or nine or ten or twelve isn't the point. The disturbing truth is that screens now command almost all our free time and attention. If we have a moment, odds are we're looking at a screen.

Let's return to the parable of the fishbowl. Not only is screen time filling the empty space in our brains, but it's also filling our schedules. Free time that used to be taken up with the Four Rs (recreation, religion, reading, and relationships) is now spent mostly alone, indoors, absorbed in the trivia served to us on our screens. Meanwhile, real life passes us by.

2.2

Why Screens Are Irresistible

There are two kinds of addiction: substance and behavioral. One can become addicted to a chemical, a habit, or both. Societies have always tried to minimize the damage addictions cause by making them socially unacceptable, illegal, and expensive.

But now there's an addictive device that's virtually free, easy to access, and so socially accepted that it's being handed to toddlers. It's actively promoted by the government, media, big business, and schools as indispensable—the very foundation of future economic progress.

That device, of course, is the glowing screen. In the previous chapter, we saw the grim statistics. Now we're going to learn how screens hijack our brains to capture our time, money, and attention.

Chirp-Ring-Buzz

In 2014, entrepreneur Kevin Holesh released a smartphone app called Moment.[1] It tracks how much time people spend using their phones. The typical Moment user picks up his or her phone thirty-nine times a day, spending almost three hours interacting with it. That's not counting the time they spend on other screens. Keep in mind that people who use Moment are the ones trying to *cut back* on screen time. Yet even these screen-aware users are spending one hundred hours a month looking at their smartphones. Over the average lifetime, that's eleven years lost to a single device.

Why do we pick up our phones so many times each day? Because they call out to us. Constantly.

Most devices ship with notifications turned on. They start chiming and buzzing the moment you put them in your pocket or purse. This is their mating call. Ignore the notifications and they pile up, making you feel as though you've missed something. Even if you don't respond, they are still distracting a part of your brain, raising your stress levels, and jolting your nervous system.

Researchers from the University of Texas recently made a startling discovery: the mere presence of a smartphone commandeers a part of your brain.[2]

In their study, three groups of volunteers were asked to put their phones in silent mode before taking a cognitive test. Group One placed their smartphones in another room, Group Two placed them in pockets or purses, and Group Three placed the phones on the desk right next to them.

The result: Group One scored highest on the test, Group Two lagged behind, and Group Three performed the worst.

How could a silenced phone have such a negative impact on mental ability? Our brains have only so much capacity to think, notice, and remember. Having a phone nearby is like a small leak in a tire, constantly draining a tiny amount of our attention and brainpower. Even when it's inert, your phone is still on your mind.

Stories abound of people having panic attacks when separated from their phones. This phenomenon has become so common that it's been given a clinical name: *nomophobia,* or fear of being without phone contact. Some mobile phone users suffer from *textaphrenia*, which involves hearing or feeling the buzz of phantom message alerts—even when their devices aren't in their purses or pockets.

We may tell ourselves we hate the way our devices constantly distract us, but our brains apparently love the stimulation. Smartphones are like miniature slot machines—buzzing and dinging at unexpected intervals, rewarding us with little dollops of novelty.

And speaking of slot machines, the companies that produce screen content are borrowing techniques from the masters of behavioral addiction: casinos.

How do casinos convince people to sit in front of slot machines hour after hour, pumping in coins (or swiping credit cards)? The answer is surprisingly simple: the machines know just how often to give the bettor a small win so he'll keep playing. Each little victory gives the gambler a dribble of dopamine, and that pleasure fools his brain into thinking he's winning, when in reality he's getting fleeced. The triumphant feelings that accompany a small win can be so intense that many gamblers don't realize they're suffering bigger losses.

The screen world has an even more insidious version of the slot machine. It's called the video game.

Every video game is designed to start the user off with a few easy wins. Over time, the game gets progressively harder, but not so difficult that the gamer quits in frustration. Along the way, he gets small rewards doled out at unexpected intervals while bigger prizes are held just out of reach.

If a player wants to succeed more quickly, he can buy power packs or upgrades that expand his character's abilities. This is why the video games industry is such a lucrative business: People pay real money to purchase artificial, on-screen goods that cost their makers nothing to distribute. With slot machines, the house wins about 52 percent of the time, but in-game purchases set the house up to win 100 percent of the time.

It's not just video games that draw us in and won't let go. Behavioral psychologists have learned that even tiny tweaks to a web page, a BUY NOW button, or a social media post can make a big difference in engagement:

> Behind the screens of the games we play and digital communities we interact with are psychologists and other behavioral science experts, who are hired to create products that we want to use more and more. Big tech now employs mental health experts to use persuasive technology, a new field of research that looks at how computers can change the way humans think and act. This technique, also known as persuasive design, is built into thousands of games and apps, and companies like Twitter, Facebook, Snapchat, Amazon, Apple, and Microsoft rely on it to encourage specific human behavior starting from a very young age.[3]

Charles Duhigg wrote a bestselling book titled *The Power of Habit* that explains how compulsions work. Duhigg says every habit can be broken down into three components: cue, routine, and reward. For example, when a smoker feels anxious (cue), he lights up a cigarette (routine). The nicotine calms his brain (reward). When a woman feels depressed (cue), she goes for a run (routine) and experiences an endorphin rush (reward).

Duhigg calls this the Habit Loop. In his book *[Un]Intentional: How Screens Secretly Shape Your Desires and How You Can Break Free*, author Doug Smith elaborates:

> So, if our boredom cue fires, our routine is to pick up our phone, because the apps have so effectively manipulated our reward system that we can't be bored—we crave the

distraction. If our loneliness cue fires, we might find a quick fix with pornography. The brain thinks, "loneliness solved, do that again."

Habits formed by screens are more dangerous because of the tight, fast, and coordinated feedback loops involved in the reward system. Where the cue-routine-reward cycle for something like food can span minutes or even hours, the same cycle is measured in milliseconds when driven by a screen.[4]

It's the instant rewards that make screen life so addictive. Never have humans been able to summon visual novelty (and the accompanying dopamine rush) so quickly, reliably, and repeatedly.

Why You Can't Stop Playing/Swiping/Watching

I want to introduce a concept you've probably never heard of: *stopping cues*. The real world is governed by stopping cues such as these:

- When the sun sets, we stop what we're doing and prepare for sleep.
- When our stomachs are full, we stop eating.
- When the final exam is over, we stop studying and apply what we've learned.
- When we arrive at our destination, we stop traveling.

In times past, the screen world had stopping cues too:

- When an episode was over, TV stations played commercials before the next program.
- Radio and TV stations signed off around midnight.
- Websites had "footers" at the bottom of every page.

- Video games were divided into levels. When a player beat a level, the game paused. When a character used up his lives, it was GAME OVER.

But the digital world is eliminating stopping cues in an effort to keep your eyeballs fixed on the screen:

- TV networks no longer schedule commercial breaks between shows. Instead, one program rolls right into the next.
- Social media and many web pages now scroll endlessly. They have no footers.
- The latest generation of games is known as "infinite format." There are no levels. The character wanders through a virtual world, and the mayhem never ceases. Characters who die "respawn" immediately. The words GAME OVER never appear.
- TV stations never sign off.

Without stopping cues, many people find it hard to tear themselves away from their screens. How many times have you started scrolling through social media, not realizing thirty minutes have passed? My gamer friends regularly play long into the night, unaware of the late hour.

■   ■   ■

The makers of screen content are not mustache-twirling villains out to destroy you. They're savvy businesspeople who earn money when you use their products and watch their programming. They exploit your natural weaknesses to keep you engaged. If you find yourself addicted to screen life, don't feel guilty. Get mad. You're being targeted by an army of sophisticated professionals whose sole job is to plug you into the Matrix and keep you there.

2.3

Phenomenal Cosmic Powers

Revolutionary new technologies amplify human power—but they also produce unintended consequences.

The bow and arrow made hunters more efficient, but also made warriors more lethal. Johannes Gutenberg's printing press sparked the Protestant Reformation, but it also plunged Europe into five centuries of political instability and war. The internal combustion engine created the explosion in wealth we enjoy today but also largely contributed to air pollution and is blamed for global warming.

We are the first generation with portable, network-connected screens—the most revolutionary communications technology ever devised. It gives us great powers, but what has it unleashed?

In this chapter, I'll be focusing on the positive. Many people (particularly young adults) don't fully appreciate the miraculous abilities screens give us. So I've written this brief chapter to put these amazing tools into perspective.

■   ■   ■

When I was an undergraduate at Baylor University in the early 1980s, the world was still mostly analog. Digital, screen-based communications platforms barely existed.

I had a roommate at Baylor named Bob, whose parents were missionaries in Uruguay. In those days, phone calls from the U.S. to Uruguay were ruinously expensive. A ten-minute conversation might cost forty dollars. However, Bob and his parents had a workaround: Every other Friday at 4:00 p.m., Bob would visit the home of a local ham operator who had a telephone patched into a shortwave radio. If the atmospheric conditions were just right, Bob could talk to his parents over a scratchy connection for free.

Bob's dad: "How's school going, son? OVER."

Bob: "Good—I did well on my English test. OVER."

Bob's mom: *GARBLED, STATIC*

Bob: "Mom, say again, OVER."

Bob's mom: "Are STATIC getting enough STATIC eat? OVER."

Bob: "Yes, Mom, my roommate David is an excellent cook! OVER."

Fast forward thirty-five years. One pleasant summer evening, my wife, Gina, and I were enjoying an after-dinner stroll. We began reminiscing about our daughter, Andrea, as we passed a patch of daisies she loved as a girl. I pulled the iPhone out of my pocket, and with a few taps I was able to identify her exact location: a grocery store near her home. I tapped a few more times, and within a minute we were connected via FaceTime. My phone showed a full-color image of her and my grandson unloading their purchases into her Subaru. Both of their voices came through loud and clear without a hint of static. She smiled brightly when I showed her the daisies.

To recap: Gina and I were walking down a rural road in Alaska while my loved ones were standing in the parking lot of a grocery store—*in Australia.* We stood on opposite sides of the globe—7,628 miles apart. We were in different hemispheres, experiencing different seasons of the year, seeing and hearing each other in real time. It was Friday evening for us; it was Saturday afternoon for her.

Folks, this is a miracle.

We take this sort of thing for granted today. As recently as 2009, this would have been impossible. Yet there I was, not even a decade later, standing outdoors, sharing real-time sounds and images with family on the other side of the world. And the call cost me nothing.

This isn't kinglike power. It's *godlike* power. No prophet, pope, or president had ever been able to do the things our screens allow us to do today.

The three powers often ascribed to deities are omnipresence, omniscience, and omnipotence. In many ways, screens grant us all three.

Omnipresence: Existing or Being Everywhere at the Same Time

Screens allow us to witness and participate in events that take place far away. I can sit in my living room in Alaska and observe high-definition color images of a rugby match taking place in South Africa. I can log on to webcams that present me with real-time images of eagles nesting in Canada, vacationers frolicking on a beach in Mexico, and rush-hour traffic in California. And yes, I can place free, two-way video calls to almost anywhere in the world.

I'm also able to project my presence to other places via screen. I can participate in meetings that take place thousands of miles away (which is very handy when one lives in Alaska). Associates can see my face, hear my voice, and watch my presentations from the other side of the globe. Doctors do the same through telemedicine, bringing healing to the sick in rural areas via screen. Teachers capture their lectures on video and release them online, allowing students to learn whenever and wherever they are able. My smart doorbell allows me to see and speak to the deliveryman on my porch even when I'm away.

Omniscience: The Capacity to Know Everything

All my screens (except my TV) can search the web for just about any tidbit of knowledge I could want. I can make myself aware of any newsworthy event happening the world over: an earthquake in Iran, labor unrest in France, septuplets born in Bangladesh. I can know the current temperature at nearly any spot on the globe, thanks to a network of more than 250,000 weather stations—many of which are maintained by volunteers. My screens can inform me of the exact time a particular flight will arrive, the score from last night's baseball game, or the daily lunch special at the eatery down the street.

Navigation is much easier today, since my phone knows just about every road on earth and can guide me turn-by-turn. But why bother to drive? A couple of taps on the phone and a car will arrive to whisk me to whatever destination I choose.

I can solve almost any equation with the built-in scientific calculator on my mobile device. If I receive a document written in Italian, my screen can translate it into English. Screens give me instant access to millions of books and online publications. The world's knowledge is vast, and I carry a good portion of it around in my pocket.

Omnipotence: Having Unlimited Power

Our screens have not yet made us omnipotent, but they have greatly expanded our powers.

Take wealth, for example. Capital used to reside in objects: coins, bills, jewels, precious metals, etc. If you wanted to transfer assets from one person or place to another, you had to physically move them (think treasure chests). Wire transfers have been around since 1872, but they were cumbersome, requiring both the sender and receiver to visit a bank or Western Union office. Today I am able to pull up a website and transfer wealth to the other side of the planet in a matter of minutes without leaving my desk.

Ancient legends told of dragons and sorcerers who could summon fire. Well, I can do that now with my smartphone. If the room's a bit chilly, I can tell Alexa to raise the temperature a degree or two. No need to chop wood or tend a hearth. I don't even have to be in the house. I can view and change the temperature in my bedroom from almost anywhere on Earth.

My screens enable me to work with talented people from all over the globe. I regularly hire announcers for my video productions via screen. I post a script online, and within hours voice actors from around the nation are auditioning for the part. A few years ago, I needed some cartoons drawn for a TV ad I was producing. I logged on to a freelancers' marketplace, put in my specifications, and went to sleep. The next morning, more than a dozen artists were vying for the job. The guy I eventually hired lives in New Zealand. He and I never actually spoke, and no physical goods changed hands between us. We transacted the entire project (communication, sketches, revisions, final drawings, and payment) via our screens.

■   ■   ■

Those of us born prior to 1990 lived in an analog world where communication and information were limited. But we've ascended to the digital throne, experiencing newfound powers—and the pressures that come with them.

Godlike powers are both a blessing and a burden. Just ask Bruce Nolan, the fictional TV reporter played by Jim Carrey in the 2003 movie *Bruce Almighty*. Bruce's career and love life were in the pits, so he cried out to God. Surprisingly, God offered to trade places with Bruce for seven days.

Suddenly, Bruce was omnipotent. He used his limitless powers to create the perfect life for himself. To boost his TV ratings, he caused a series of miracles and disasters to occur just as he was covering mundane news events. He humiliated his workplace rival and took over the news anchor's chair. And in an effort to seduce his girlfriend, Bruce pulled the moon out of its orbit and brought it closer to Earth. Meanwhile, he was bombarded with millions of prayer requests from all over the planet. Completely overwhelmed, he set his computer to answer every prayer with "Yes."

Chaos ensued. The miracles caused panic as millions believed the apocalypse was nigh. The sudden increase in the moon's gravity caused tsunamis. Tens of thousands of people won the lottery, driving the jackpot down to seventeen dollars each. And to top things off, Bruce got dumped by his girlfriend.

In the end, Bruce realized that unlimited power was served with a side dish of crushing pressure. He fell to his knees, begging God to take back his powers. Bruce looked up and saw a shimmering light: the headlights of an oncoming truck.

As we stare into the luminous faces of our screens, we're beginning to realize the danger headed our way. You may not feel like your screens have given you godlike powers. In fact, you may feel weaker than ever: bombarded by emails and online trolls, stressed out by FOMO, and painfully aware of the many ways you don't measure up to the glamorous people and perfect lives you see on screen. Your job may have been taken by a computer—or your employer may insist you work from everywhere, on call 24/7. You may feel less than divine as your relationships atrophy and loneliness bears down on your soul.

The same screens that multiplied our powers are ultimately confining us. The genie in Disney's animated feature *Aladdin* described our digital dilemma perfectly: PHENOMENAL COSMIC POWERS!—*itty bitty living space.*

2.4

How Screens Are Conquering Youthful Rebellion

There are dozens of books and web resources warning parents about their kids', tweens', and teens' screen use. I read a bunch of them. They will make you want to bury your screens in the backyard and move to an Amish community.

But the news isn't all bad. Screens seem to be making our kids physically safer, which is a good thing. However, that safety comes at a cost.

■   ■   ■

There have always been rebellious teens and young adults, particularly among the upper classes. King David's son Absalom rose up against him. Romeo and Juliet fell in love against their parents' wishes. One of Jesus's most famous parables tells of a prodigal son who blew half his father's fortune on wild parties.

But historically speaking, teens have always been too poor, busy, and exhausted to raise much of a ruckus. Most children began working alongside their parents at a young age. They married and started families in their teens. There simply wasn't the time or money to get into much trouble.

But this changed with the advent of child labor laws and compulsory education. Youngsters suddenly had leisure time on their hands, and during the twentieth century, rates of youth crime, substance abuse, and teen pregnancy all rose in the developed world. Idle hands truly were the devil's workshop.

Then something completely unexpected happened. Toward the end of the twentieth century, many of these negative trends began reversing themselves. Sociologists were stunned. Were young people suddenly making better choices, or was something else causing kids to turn their backs on youthful rebellion?

Dr. Jean Twenge may have found the answer. She's the author of *iGen: Why Today's Super-Connected Kids Are Growing Up Less Rebellious, More Tolerant, Less Happy—and Completely Unprepared for Adulthood* (there's actually more to the title, but I clipped it in the interest of brevity).[1]

iGen (which includes people born between 1995 and 2012) is the first generation to grow up with always-on wireless broadband internet (hence the name iGen). As such, these digital natives have never known a world without interactive screen content. They number some seventy-four million, or a little less than a quarter of the U.S. population.

Twenge is a social scientist who crunched a large amount of data in preparing her book. She compared iGen to previous generations, looking for trends. What she saw alarmed her, particularly the spike in depression and suicide around 2012—the year smartphones became ubiquitous among teens and young adults.

However, Twenge also found a number of trends that would warm the heart of any parent, teacher, or minister.

First and most striking: iGen has stepped back from the risky, rebellious behaviors members of my generation (Boomers) engaged in to establish our independence. Rather than growing up too fast, iGen is growing up exceptionally slowly. They are expanding the boundaries of childhood, maturing later, and prolonging adolescence into their twenties. Record numbers are living with their parents well into adulthood.

iGen tends to hang out with parents as much or more than with friends. And they're homebodies. They barely leave the house compared to the generations that preceded them. Twenge writes:

> The numbers are stunning: twelfth-graders in 2015 are going out less often than eighth-graders did as recently as 2009. So eighteen-year-olds are now going out less often than fourteen-year-olds did just six years prior.

Maybe one reason they're not going out is because they can't drive. In 2015, for the first time in decades, the majority of tenth graders in the U.S. possessed neither a license nor a learner's permit. Many are content to be driven here and there by parents, and many moms and dads seem happy to chauffeur.

iGen teens are also kissing dating goodbye. Only about half as many iGen high school seniors go out on dates as their Generation X and Baby Boomer parents. They are also less sexually active than their predecessors. Kate Julian writes in *The Atlantic*:[2]

> To the relief of many parents, educators, and clergy members who care about the health and well-being of young people, teens are launching their sex lives later.[3] From 1991 to 2017, the Centers for Disease Control and Prevention's Youth Risk Behavior Survey finds the *percentage of high-school students*

who'd had intercourse dropped from 54 to 40 percent.[4] In other words, in the space of a generation, sex has gone from something most high-school students have experienced to something most haven't.

It's not just teens; everyone's having less sex these days. Julian calls it part of "the sex recession." The teen birth rate has hit an all-time low, as has the overall abortion rate in the developed world.[5]

iGen is also less likely to booze it up. Binge drinking by high school seniors has been cut in half since the 1990s. Twenge writes, "Nearly 40 percent of iGen high school seniors in 2016 had never tried alcohol at all, and the number of eighth-graders who have tried alcohol has been cut nearly in half. The decline in trying alcohol is the largest in the youngest groups and by far the smallest among young adults."

Schoolyard brawls were common when I was a boy, but they're a dying ritual today. In 1991, half of ninth-graders had been in a physical fight, but by 2015, only a quarter had. The homicide rate among teens and young adults reached a forty-year low in 2014. Fewer teens are carrying weapons to school. And despite all the attention sexual misconduct gets in the media, rates of campus rape and assault fell by more than half between 1997 and 2013.

Twenge takes pains to note that these trends are not merely the province of upper middle–class whites. "Youths of every racial group, region, and class are growing up more slowly," she says. She also points out that fewer iGens are holding jobs, volunteering, or participating in extracurricular activities. They also spend less time doing homework and are less likely to attend church or youth group.

As Twenge puts it, "No matter what the reason, teens are growing up more slowly, eschewing adult activities until they are older. This creates a logical question: If teens are working less, spending less time on homework, going out less, and drinking less, what are they doing?

For a generation called iGen, the answer is obvious: look no further than the smartphones in their hands."

Kids are getting into less trouble because they're much less likely to physically gather. Having fewer interpersonal interactions reduces the pressure to do stupid things and minimizes the chance of conflict or physical injury. You can't give someone a bloody nose on Twitter, and nobody's ever gotten pregnant over a broadband connection.

In addition, screens have made staying at home a lot more entertaining than going out. Why go to the movies and pay to see one flick when Mom and Dad's living room has a seventy-inch flat-screen TV, complete with 5.1 surround sound and thousands of on-demand programs to watch? There's no need to drop quarters at the local video arcade—simply fire up your Xbox and play the most sophisticated games ever created. And why hang out at the mall when your friends are hanging out online?

Young people are forging new ways of interacting with the world. Their identities increasingly exist in cyberspace, giving them much less incentive to intermingle face-to-face. We've spent a century trying to make our kids safer, and if fewer teens are out on the streets at night making mischief, most of us would cry "Hallelujah!"

But as the title of Twenge's book says, kids are growing up "less happy" and "completely unprepared for adulthood." Screen life has tossed a blanket of physical protection over our kids while stunting their emotional resilience. Having spent the bulk of their free time in the screen world, many youngsters are reaching adulthood unsure of how to master the real world.

2.5

Sleepier, Fatter, and Sicker: What Screens Are Doing to Our Bodies

For the most part, screen life has been a disaster for our bodies. Let's start by looking at the bathroom scale.

In 1960, when the television age had just begun in the U.S., the average adult woman in America weighed 140 pounds, and the average man weighed 166. Fifty-five years later, women weighed 166, and men weighed 196. In other words, the typical woman in 2015 weighed as much as the typical man did in 1960.[1]

Why did both men and women get 18 percent heavier in just fifty-five years? Doctors blame four things: 1) the rise of calorie-dense processed foods, 2) sedentary jobs, 3) labor-saving devices such as washing machines and powered garage door openers, and 4) a huge increase in chair-bound screen time.

Our screens may not be the only reason we've gotten chunky, but they are the primary reason we're staying that way. TV's predecessor, radio, allowed us to stay active while we listened. But television immobilized our bodies, requiring us to sit still and lock our eyes, at least until a commercial break came along. Then in the 1980s, four new technologies emerged that turned us into true couch potatoes:

- In the post-Apollo era, NASA turned its attention to launching communication satellites, which in turn facilitated an explosion of basic cable channels (CNN, MTV, ESPN, USA, etc.). The number of basic cable subscribers in the U.S. more than tripled during the 1980s.[2]
- VCRs and video rentals eliminated commercial breaks, keeping us glued to the sofa for hours at a time.
- The Nintendo Entertainment System popularized home video gaming.
- And worst of all: in 1980, a Canadian company called Viewstar introduced the first infrared wireless remote, enabling viewers to control every feature on their TVs and VCRs from the comfort of their La-Z-Boys.[3]

All this immobility increased our girth, which in turn took a huge toll on overall health, even among children. Dr. Victoria Dunckley writes:

> In general, screen-time is associated with weight gain, high blood pressure, blood sugar dysregulation, and high cholesterol. Further, studies suggest screen-time increases risk for cardiovascular disease, diabetes, and metabolic syndrome—conditions that were essentially unheard of in children even one generation ago.
>
> In addition, studies suggest that screen-time slows metabolism and impairs hunger and fullness cues, leading to overeating and weight gain. In fact, screen-time is associated with obesity regardless of physical activity, suggesting

it has effects outside of simply displacing more physically active play.[4]

But if screens made us heavier in the past, they're trying to make us skinny again now. TVs began showing up in gyms in the 1990s, making treadmill time less boring. Many home exercise machines have a tablet holder or a built-in screen to entertain you while you sweat. Fitness apps guide our workouts and encourage outdoor walking. The fitness trackers on our wrists send us messages throughout the day, reminding us to stand up and keep moving. And smart TVs allow us to stream personal-training videos directly into our living rooms.

Sleep under Siege

In 1942, about a decade before televisions began invading our homes, the average American slept about 7.9 hours a night. By 2013, that number had fallen to 6.8 hours a night.[5] According to a Gallup poll, 43 percent of Americans say they would feel better if they got more sleep. And they're right. Lack of sleep puts you at risk for a host of health problems, including heart disease, high blood pressure, stroke, and diabetes. It can lower your libido and testosterone. Sleeplessness can make you fuzzy-headed, forgetful, and prone to depression. It can even make you less attractive:

> When you don't get enough sleep, your body releases more of the stress hormone cortisol. In excess amounts, cortisol can break down skin collagen, the protein that keeps skin smooth and elastic.
>
> When it comes to body weight, it may be that if you snooze, you lose. Lack of sleep seems to be related to an increase in hunger and appetite, and possibly to obesity. According to a 2004 study, people who sleep less than six

hours a day were almost 30 percent more likely to become obese than those who slept seven to nine hours.[6]

We need our beauty sleep, so why aren't we getting it? Screens keep us awake even after we feel sleepy. It's more fun to stimulate your brain than relax it. Carolyn Y. Johnson writes in the *Washington Post*:

> "It used to be popular for people to say, 'I'll sleep when I'm dead.' The ironic thing is, not sleeping enough may get you there sooner," said Daniel Buysse, a professor of sleep medicine at the University of Pittsburgh.
>
> In the screen-lit bustle of modern life, sleep is expendable. There are television shows to binge-watch, work emails to answer, homework to finish, social media posts to scroll through. We'll catch up on shut-eye later, so the thinking goes—right after we click down one last digital rabbit hole.
>
> An alarming new line of research suggests poor sleep may increase the risk of Alzheimer's, as even a single night of sleep deprivation boosts brain levels of the proteins that form toxic clumps in Alzheimer's patients. All-nighters push anxiety to clinical levels, and even modest sleep reductions are linked to increased feelings of social isolation and loneliness.[7]

Younger Americans are more prone to sleeplessness than Americans fifty and older. In 2019, Common Sense Media released an extensive study titled "The New Normal: Parents, Teens, Screens, and Sleep in the United States."[8] Here are some key findings:

1. Parents and teens keep their mobile devices close by at night. Sixty-two percent of parents charge their mobile phones within reach of the bed, compared to 39 percent of children (age eight to eighteen).

2. Twenty-nine percent of kids sleep with their phones. Girls take their devices to bed more than boys (33 versus 26 percent).

3. Mobile devices are interrupting our sleep. Thirty-six percent of teens wake up and check their mobile devices for something other than the time at least once a night. Twenty-six percent of parents do this as well. Parents look at their phones to check notifications (51 percent) or due to insomnia (48 percent). Kids wake up at night because they've received a notification (54 percent) or they want to check on their social media posts (51 percent).

4. Both parents and kids regularly use screens in the hour before bed, even though doctors say this disrupts our sleep. A majority of parents (61 percent) and kids (70 percent) use their devices within thirty minutes of going to bed.

5. Two-thirds of teens are on their devices within thirty minutes of waking up (not counting using it as an alarm clock). Thirty-two percent check it within five minutes of waking.

Screens disrupt our sleep in three main ways:

1. They keep us up late watching TV and videos, texting, answering emails, surfing, checking social media, etc.

2. Our devices chirp, ring, and vibrate all night with notifications. Even if we sleep right through these stimuli, evidence suggests they may rouse us just enough to interrupt our natural sleep cycle, leaving us feeling fatigued the next day.

3. All screens emit artificial blue-tinted light, which tricks our brains into thinking it's daytime.

The Problem with Blue Light

Prior to Thomas Edison's invention of the light bulb in 1879, there were only three sources of persistent light on earth: sunlight, moonlight, and fire. Each of these illumination sources has a different *color temperature:*

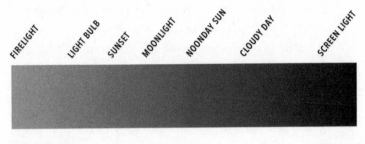

MORE ORANGE   **MORE BLUE**

Natural daylight has a blue tint to it, although you don't notice it. But as the sun sets, the sky takes on a more orange hue. Believe it or not, moonlight is also more orange than full daylight (the blue shift is an optical illusion). Firelight is even more orange.

As the light entering our eyes shifts toward orange, the brain's pineal gland begins to produce melatonin, a natural hormone that makes us sleepy. But blue light suppresses melatonin production, since our brains think it's daytime.

The light from Edison's bulb gives off an orange glow, so it has never interfered much with our sleep. But in the 1950s, televisions began producing bluish light at night for the first time. TV sets and computer monitors emit extremely blue light, similar to looking at a clear blue sky with the sun at your back. Viewing a screen at 11:00 p.m. tells your brain it's high noon. That's one reason doctors recommend we turn off our screens at least an hour before we go to bed. (There is a workaround for the blue light problem. I discuss it in Chapter 3.3.) Doctors also recommend that adults and children not use any form of interactive media before bed because of its highly stimulating effect on the brain.

Tired, Damaged Eyes

Nothing in nature emits constant, bright light like a screen. Staring at a glowing object for long periods of time is unnatural and can cause eye strain or even permanent damage. Doctors call this Computer Vision Syndrome. Symptoms can include blurred vision, double vision, dryness, red eyes, headaches, and neck pain. And although your brain can't perceive it, your screens are rapidly flashing at you (this is called refresh rate), which is also unnatural to the eye:

> When you work at a computer, your eyes have to focus and refocus all the time. They move back and forth as you read. You may have to look down at papers and then back up to type. Your eyes react to images constantly moving and changing, shifting focus, sending rapidly varying images to the brain. All these jobs require a lot of effort from your eye muscles. And to make things worse, unlike a book or piece of paper, the screen adds contrast, flicker, and glare. What's more, it is proven that we blink far less frequently when using a computer, which causes the eyes to dry out and blur your vision periodically while working.[9]

Excessive screen time may be damaging young eyes. Since the 1970s, the percentage of American children who need corrective lenses has nearly doubled. Children who spend long hours staring at screens are at increased risk of developing myopia, or short-sightedness.[10]

Physical Injury

Children and adults who use screens excessively may actually injure themselves. Heavy texters and habitual gamers are developing carpal tunnel syndrome and tendinitis from holding their devices for hours on end. Virtual Reality gamers, blinded to real-world hazards by their headsets, are tripping, falling, and colliding with objects, particularly as their arms flail in all directions. Some outdoor augmented reality gamers (using phone apps such as Pokémon Go) have walked right into oncoming traffic. And speaking of traffic, texting while driving contributes to 1.6 million auto accidents a year, resulting in half a million injuries.[11]

Our heads are meant to look forward, but staring down at our screens is causing a new syndrome called "text neck." Lindsey Bever writes in the *Washington Post*:[12]

> The human head weighs about a dozen pounds. But as the neck bends forward and down, the weight on the cervical spine begins to increase. At a 15-degree angle, this weight is about 27 pounds, at 30 degrees it's 40 pounds, at 45 degrees it's 49 pounds, and at 60 degrees it's 60 pounds.
>
> That's the burden that comes with staring at a smartphone—the way millions do for hours every day, according to research published by Kenneth Hansraj in the National Library of Medicine.[13] Over time, researchers say, this poor posture, sometimes called "text neck," can lead to early wear-and-tear on the spine, degeneration and even surgery.

During the COVID-19 lockdowns, chiropractors reported an uptick in patients reporting pain from spending hours slumping on the couch in front of laptops, TVs, and smartphones. "You think you are getting all comfortable by sitting in a comfy chair, putting the laptop on a pillow and your legs on an ottoman. But then after sitting that way through a ninety-minute Zoom meeting, it turns out you are laying waste to your spine," said Boston businessman Anthony Flint.[14]

Screen life has been very bad for our bodies, but that's nothing compared to what it's done to our minds. I'll share my own brain-impairment story in our next chapter.

2.6

What Screens Are Doing to Our Brains

When I began researching this book about a year ago, I purchased five screen-related books to bone up on the topic. I picked up the first one, settled into my easy chair, parked my glasses on my nose, and started to read, highlighter in hand.

After about an hour, I had managed to read just eleven pages. This shocked me. I've always been a fast reader. I went back to reading and began to notice something odd. After every paragraph or two, I'd look around the room, adjust my glasses, or stop to think about something. I also stood up and took three breaks during that second hour.

Then it occurred to me: I hadn't sat down and read an entire book—paper or e-reader—in about a year. All of my reading had been online, primarily short articles on news sites or posts on social media. I had trained my brain to read in short bursts, darting from screen to screen, topic to topic, spending an average of two to three minutes before it was off to the next article. Social media had made things even worse. I typically spend less than five seconds on a post before scrolling down in search of more novelty to keep my brain stimulated.

So when I sat down and tried to read that first book, my brain rebelled. It had come to expect incessant novelty, but it was getting monotony, which my mind interpreted as an abnormal experience. In response, my body tried to create novelty by fidgeting, looking around, getting up, and pausing to think and daydream. I don't know if years of web surfing has altered the structure of my brain, but it has certainly made it more prone to distraction.

I'm happy to say that after reading those five books, my ability to concentrate came back—perhaps not as strongly as before, but there was noticeable improvement. And writing this book has been one of the most restorative tasks I could have undertaken. I could almost feel the neural pathways in my brain reopening as I concentrated on a single task.

But what about children whose still-developing brains are being altered by screen time? Will they ever be able to concentrate, or will the damage be permanent?

The Incredible Shrinking Brain

We've known for decades that excessive TV viewing is linked to shorter attention spans, poor eating habits, and disciplinary problems in children. Excessive interactive screen time has also been implicated in language delay, sleep disorders, and decreased parent-child interaction. But are these negative outcomes a result of a change in our brains? Sandee LaMotte writes:

> Screen time use by infants, toddlers, and preschoolers has exploded over the last decade, concerning experts about the impact of television, tablets, and smartphones on these critical years of rapid brain development.
>
> Now a new study scanned the brains of children three to five years old and found those who used screens more

than the recommended one hour a day without parental involvement had lower levels of development in the brain's white matter—an area key to the development of language, literacy, and cognitive skills.[1]

Dr. John Hutton, lead author of the report, was especially concerned about the young age at which kids were being exposed to screens. "About 90 percent are using screens by age one," he said. "We've done some studies where kids are using them by two months old.

"This is important because the brain is developing the most rapidly in the first five years," Hutton said. "That's when brains are very plastic and soaking up everything, forming these strong connections that last for life."

Hutton doesn't believe that screen time itself damages the brain's white matter. "Perhaps screen time got in the way of other experiences that could have helped the children reinforce these brain networks more strongly," he said. In other words, filling a child's brain with screen time is like overfilling the fishbowl with water, displacing the balls that are vital to a child's cognitive development. Sandee LaMotte continues:

> In addition to the MRI results, excessive screen time was significantly associated with poorer emerging literacy skills and ability to use expressive language, as well as testing lower on the ability to rapidly name objects on cognitive tests taken by the forty-seven children in the study.

Heavy screen users actually experience brain shrinkage—especially teens and young adults whose gray matter is still forming.[2] Young people who use screens more than seven hours a day (a fairly typical number for many American teens) are more than twice as likely to be diagnosed with depression or anxiety as those who use screens for an hour a day or less. Heavy screen users were more easily distracted, less emotionally stable, and had more difficulty finishing tasks and making friends.[3]

Want your kid to fall behind in school? Give her a bunch of screen time as a toddler. Dr. Nicholas Kardaras is one of the world's foremost experts on kids and digital addiction. He writes:

> Brain-imaging research is showing that glowing screens— like those of iPads—are as stimulating to the brain's pleasure center and as able to increase levels of dopamine (the primary feel-good neurotransmitter) as much as sex does. This brain-orgasm effect is what makes screens so addictive for adults, but even more so for children with still-developing brains that just aren't equipped to handle that level of stimulation.
>
> What's more, an ever-increasing amount of clinical research correlates screen tech with psychiatric disorders like ADHD, addiction, anxiety, depression, increased aggression and even psychosis. Perhaps the most shocking of all, recent brain-imaging studies conclusively show that excessive screen exposure can neurologically damage a young person's developing brain in the same way that cocaine addiction can.
>
> That's right—a kid's brain on tech looks like a brain on drugs.[4]

Dr. Peter Whybrow, director of neurosciences at UCLA, calls screens "electronic cocaine." Brain imaging research shows that interactive screen content "affects the brain's frontal cortex, which controls executive functioning and impulse control the same way cocaine does. Technology is so hyper-arousing that it raises dopamine levels—the feel-good neurotransmitter most involved in the addiction dynamic." Dr. Whybrow compares the level of arousal to having sex.[5]

ADHD stands for attention-deficit/hyperactivity disorder. Individuals with ADHD have trouble paying attention, tend to be fidgety and hyperactive, and tend to make impulsive decisions without thinking through the consequences. Between 1997 and 2016, the percentage of children and adolescents in the U.S. who were diagnosed with ADHD increased from 6.1 percent to 10.2 percent.[6] Boys continue to be diagnosed with ADHD at rates far exceeding girls, although girls are catching up.

Why did ADHD diagnoses nearly double in twenty years? Increased interactive screen time may be a factor. Dr. Joshua Rosenblatt writes:[7]

> The next time you think about passing your preschooler a smartphone or tablet at the dinner table to keep them entertained, you might want to think twice.
>
> A new study out of the University of Alberta has found that by the age of 5, children who spent two hours or more looking at a screen each day were 7.7 times more likely to meet the criteria for a diagnosis of attention deficit hyperactivity disorder (ADHD) when compared to children who spent 30 minutes or less each day on a screen.

Recall the story of David the shepherd boy. That parable taught us that monotony has always been normal; novelty has always been rare. Monotony calms the brain while novelty riles it up.

But interactive screen content is turning this ancient reality on its head. Our screen-absorbed children are habituating to a world where novelty is normal and monotony feels abnormal. Low-stimulation situations like sitting and listening, reading quietly, or concentrating on a project feel wrong. The screen-habituated child will attempt to create novelty by wiggling, looking around the room, or acting out.

Mikey was an elementary school student who had been diagnosed with mild autism and ADHD. Mikey refused to do homework and flew into a rage almost every school day, throwing chairs and knocking over his desk. At home he spent many hours immersed in cartoon shows and video games.

Mikey's parents talked to a psychologist who recommended a four-week electronic screen fast. Mikey's parents eliminated all screen time and bought him Legos and puzzles. They scheduled park outings to re-immerse him in real life. Almost immediately, Mikey's tantrums and ADHD symptoms disappeared. The boy who had daily meltdowns went an entire year without a single act of aggression.

In describing the case, Dr. Kardaras writes, "In ninety-nine cases out of 100, a boy behaving this way would have invariably been put on strong psychotropic medication and perhaps even sedating antipsychotic meds." He continues, "All that was required was a removal of the hyperstimulating screens that were raising his arousal thermostat to the point where he couldn't shut it off." Dr. Kardaras reports that 90 percent of the students he has worked with who have been classified with either an attentional, behavioral, emotional, or developmental problem also had a problematic relationship with screens. Their condition typically improves the moment their screen time becomes limited.[8]

Passive versus Interactive Screen Time

There are two types of screen time: passive (lean-back) and interactive (lean-forward). Both can be beneficial or harmful, depending on how and how much we use them.

Prior to the 1970s, all screen use was passive. The moviegoer or television watcher leaned back, sat inert, and watched what was presented on the screen. The viewer did not interact with the screen content and had no control over what was presented (other than changing the volume or channel). This is still the case today when we watch a TV show or movie. We don't decide what happens on the screen. The audience's job is to lean back and absorb the content as presented by the filmmaker.

But with the introduction of video games in 1972, screen content became interactive for the first time. The user manipulates what he sees on the screen. That can mean controlling an on-screen character who travels through simulated three-dimensional space. It can also involve solving a puzzle or building a virtual world.

The personal-computing revolution of the 1980s introduced interactive screen life to the masses. Millions learned to alter and create screen content via keyboard and mouse. The World Wide Web allowed users to click on hyperlinks, watch video clips, and purchase items online. Social media granted individuals the ability to post, react, and share thoughts online. Mobile devices made interactive screen time an anywhere-anytime experience.

Passive (lean-back) screen activities	Interactive (lean-forward) screen activities
Watching TV	Web surfing via hyperlinks
Going to a movie	Social media
Streaming videos	Texting and email
Video chatting	Computer work and creative pursuits
	Video gaming

Passive or Interactive: Which Affects Us More?

Dr. Victoria Dunckley says both passive and interactive screen time are associated with a host of negative outcomes, including attention problems, depression, sleep disorders, irritability, and diminished creativity. However, interactive screen time is more stimulating to the brain. And therein lies the danger, particularly when it comes to children. She writes:

> A 2012 study surveying the habits of over two thousand kindergarten, elementary, and junior high school children found that the minimum amount of screen-time associated with sleep disturbance was just thirty minutes for interactive (computer or video game use) compared to two hours for passive (television use). A 2007 study demonstrated that sleep and memory were significantly impaired following a single session of excessive computer game playing, while a single session of excessive television viewing produced only mild sleep impairment and had no effect on memory. And a large 2011 survey of American adolescents and adults demonstrated that interactive device use before bedtime was strongly associated with trouble falling asleep and staying asleep while passive media use was not.[9]

Both passive and interactive screen content rev up the brain. But interactive content works the brain harder because the viewer is controlling what happens on the screen. Passive screen time is like visiting an art gallery and viewing a collection of paintings. Interactive screen time is like picking up a brush and painting your own masterpiece. Which requires more brain power?

During a two-hour session of passive screen time (such as watching a movie), the viewer's brain does experience stimulation by following the storyline, processing the dialogue, and witnessing the constantly changing images. However, the higher-level decision-making centers of the brain hardly fire at all.

But during a two-hour stint with interactive media, the user makes hundreds or even thousands of little micro-decisions. *Which link do I visit? How do I respond to a friend's post? Where do I find more ammo before the aliens kill me?* Interactive media requires a lot more brain power—while delivering greater dopamine rewards. That's why it's become so much more addicting and mood-altering than passive media ever was.

Ironically, many parents limit lean-back screen activities like watching TV because they associate it with laziness. However, they let their kids have as much lean-forward screen time as they want because they see it as stimulating. In reality, parents should sharply restrict lean-forward screen time because of its potential to overstimulate the brain but allow their children a carefully monitored amount of lean-back screen use as appropriate. And just how much is appropriate? Probably less than they're getting now. I'll offer some recommendations in Chapter 4.1.

2.7

Screens = Anxiety Machines

Jelena Kecmanovic is a clinical psychologist who practices in suburban Washington, D.C. And like many psychologists, therapists, and counselors, she sees a rising tide of anxiety among her patients:

> We live in the age of anxiety. As a psychologist who has studied anxiety and treated hundreds of anxious patients, I see it eclipsing all other problems as a major psychological issue in the twenty-first century. Each day, I treat people who worry constantly and can't relax, who feel tense and achy, and who have difficulty sleeping—all hallmarks of anxiety. Survey data confirm anxiety is ubiquitous.
>
> Living in the developed world does not typically bring us into constant contact with life-threatening danger. But our threat-detection system remains vigilant, and it's being bombarded like never before.[1]

Our great-grandparents never seemed this anxious as they dealt with famine, pandemics, the horrors of two world wars, the Great Depression, the threat of nuclear annihilation, assassinations, rioting, and terrorist attacks. Why are we so much more fragile today? The reasons are many, but they are all rooted in the same technology: screens and everything they place in front of us.

Choices, Choices

Ironically, one of the primary reasons we are so anxious is because our screens present us with so many wonderful choices. We're afraid to make the wrong one. Derek Thompson writes in *The Atlantic*:

> Gone are the days when young generations inherited religions and occupations and life paths from their parents as if they were unalterable strands of DNA. This is the age of DIY-everything, in which individuals are charged with the full-service construction of their careers, lives, faiths, and public identities.... All the forces of maximal freedom are also forces of anxiety, because anybody who feels obligated to select the ingredients of a perfect life from an infinite menu of options may feel lost in the infinitude.[2]

Maximal freedom creates anxiety because choice is a relatively new phenomenon. To illustrate, let's revisit David the shepherd boy. He spent his formative years as a commoner, as have 99 percent of the people who have ever lived. The commoner's "menu of options" was essentially blank. Common folk spent their lives in the same settlement among the same people. Their marriages were arranged. They followed their parents into a trade, and even their surnames were determined by their occupation: Baker, Smith, Carpenter, Wright. This choiceless existence is the normal state of human affairs.

But when David became king, he suddenly faced a multiplicity of choices, and every one of them affected his people, position, and power. All these options brought on a new kind of anxiety he had rarely experienced as a shepherd: *fear of making the wrong choice.* Today we all experience option overload and the anxiety that goes with it. David Brooks writes in the *New York Times*:

> Americans now have more choices over more things than any other culture in human history. We can choose between a broader array of foods, media sources, lifestyles and identities. We have more freedom to live out our own sexual identities and more religious and nonreligious options to express our spiritual natures.[3]

Screens are the enchanted portal that present these choices to us. But when faced with so many options, some young adults are simply choosing not to choose. Millennials are famously commitment-phobic, even in the small things. They're notorious for not making weekend plans until the very last moment, for not joining clubs and organizations, and not showing up because "something else came up." They're the "spiritual but not religious" generation—they love God but see little value in joining a church. Young adults are postponing marriage, home ownership, and career pursuits in part because they've been presented with so many options via their screens. Dr. Deb Knobelman says, "We put off making decisions because we are obsessed with making the perfect one."[4]

News: We're All Gonna Die!

There's always been bad news in our world, but we've never known 99 percent of it. Five hundred years ago, a resident of Ireland never would have heard about a plague in South America, civil unrest in Africa, or a deadly typhoon in the Philippines. As shipping increased in the seventeenth century, news accounts started to creep slowly around the world, and newspapers began reporting these crises. But there were no pictures, so the devastation was hard to imagine.

But in the 1910s, newsreels began capturing footage of world events. As moviegoers settled into their seats, they saw moving images of tragedies such as World War I, the Spanish Flu epidemic, and the great Soviet famine. Audiences were both fascinated and appalled as they witnessed the vast scope of human suffering for the first time.

These disquieting images began trickling into our homes with the advent of television news in the late 1940s. Vietnam was the first war to be broadcast into America's living rooms, and the nightly reports showing mangled bodies and flag-draped coffins were widely credited (or blamed) with fueling the 1960s anti-war movement.

For decades, Americans got an hour of TV news each day: thirty minutes of national, thirty minutes of local, always at dinnertime. Then it was back to mindless entertainment like *Batman*, *Gilligan's Island*, and *Hawaii Five-0*. Sixty minutes with the wolf was manageable. Scary, but not overwhelming.

Then in 1980, a cable TV mogul from Atlanta changed the world forever. Ted Turner launched Cable News Network, or CNN—and the twenty-four-hour news cycle was born.

For the first time, the news never stopped. CNN pushed an endless stream of controversy, crisis, and conflict into America's living rooms. Images of wars, floods, famines, and epidemics became our constant companions. Stories of dishonest businessmen, corrupt politicians, unfaithful spouses, and disgraced clerics slowly eroded trust in our leaders and institutions. Crime waves, drug epidemics, gang violence, environmental catastrophes—the only escape was to change the channel.

As news outlets proliferated on cable TV and the internet, the competition for eyeballs intensified. Sites trotted out new wolves every few minutes to keep us clicking, reading, and panicking.

All these wolves snarling at us twenty-four hours a day have convinced us we live in a world that's spiraling toward its doom. A majority of residents in fourteen of the world's most peaceful and prosperous nations believe the world is getting worse, not better. But this is precisely the opposite of reality. We live in a time of unmatched peace and prosperity. Joshua Rothman writes in *The Atlantic*:

> Despite our dark imaginings, life has been getting better in pretty much every way. Around the globe, improved health care has dramatically reduced infant and maternal mortality, and children are now better fed, better educated, and less abused. Workers make more money, are injured less frequently, and retire earlier. In the United States, fewer people are poor, while elsewhere in the world, and especially in Asia, billions fewer live in extreme poverty, defined as an income of less than a dollar and ninety cents per day. Statistics show that the world is growing less polluted and has more parks and protected wilderness. "Carbon intensity"—the amount of carbon released per dollar of GDP—has also been falling almost everywhere, a sign that we may be capable of addressing our two biggest challenges, poverty and climate change, simultaneously.[5]

The world may be experiencing moral decay, but from a material and public-health perspective, life is undoubtedly getting better. That leaves just one thing left to frighten us: the end of the world.

These days one can hardly pick up a newspaper, watch TV news, or surf the web without encountering dire warnings about the impending "climate catastrophe." All the smart people believe that climate change will result in massive suffering, if not the end of humanity itself. So certain are we of our imminent doom that legions of young adults are swearing off childbearing, and schoolchildren are experiencing panic attacks. Climate change is the media's most resilient wolf yet, since any unusual weather occurrence (be it hot or cold, wet or dry, windy or still) can be reported as evidence of a deteriorating atmosphere.

As I mentioned in the introduction, I am completing this book as the COVID-19 pandemic is spreading across the globe. Many media outlets are hyping the peril while failing to put the disease's impact in perspective. Particularly egregious is the *Washington Post*.

Here is a headline from its online edition on April 12, 2020: "'It Feels Like a War Zone': As More of Them Die, Grocery Workers Increasingly Fear Showing Up at Work."[6]

Based on this headline, I pictured frozen-food aisles stacked with corpses. But at the time this story ran, COVID-19 had killed one out of every 31,700 grocery workers. As a comparison, one out of every 106 Americans will die in a car crash.

Here's another from the *Post* from April 8, 2020: "Hundreds of Young Americans Have Now Been Killed by the Coronavirus, Data Shows. ER Doctor: 'Just Because They Are Young Doesn't Mean They Aren't Vulnerable'"[7]

And what does that data show? At the time of its publication, 255 Americans under 40 were known to have died of the disease. Compared to the total U.S. population, that's less than one in a million.

And here's one more headline from the *Post*, dated April 25, 2020: "Young and Middle-Aged People, Barely Sick with Covid-19, Are Dying of Strokes."[8] The subtitle says, "Doctors sound alarm about patients in their 30s and 40s left debilitated or dead. Some didn't even know they were infected."

A survey of fourteen regional medical centers identified a total of five people under age fifty who suffered COVID-related strokes. Only one died. *One.* That frightening headline made it sound as if dozens of healthy young adults with no symptoms were suddenly collapsing face-first into their cappuccinos.

Here's the game the media play: they don't lie, but they present the truth with a heavy dose of spin and sensationalism. There's a name for this: *yellow journalism*. The scarier the wolf, the more we pay attention. Attention equals more advertising revenue.

I'm not saying that threats such as pandemics or climate change are not dire or real. Here's my point: In an era of unprecedented peace, prosperity, and progress, our screens are blinding us to how good we have it. They are making us believe the world is a dangerous hellscape while stoking conflict and pitting us against each other. Next stop: the Matrix.

Thou Shalt Covet

Back to David the shepherd boy. As a young Hebrew, he would have known the Ten Commandments by heart. The last one says:

> You shall not covet your neighbor's house; you shall not covet your neighbor's wife, or his male servant, or his female servant, or his ox, or his donkey, or anything that is your neighbor's.

In David's day, there wasn't that much to covet. House. Spouse. Servants. Livestock. It's a short list. But today, screens present us with plenty to covet, including sleek automobiles, fashionable clothing, dream homes, and luxury vacations. In the 1970s, the average American was exposed to about five hundred advertisements per day. Today, that number is approaching five thousand.[9]

The rich used to keep their affluence under wraps. It was considered poor taste to flaunt one's wealth. But in the 1980s, a popular television show called *Lifestyles of the Rich and Famous* pierced that veil, taking viewers inside the opulent private worlds of successful entertainers, tycoons, and athletes. During that same era, rap musicians began flaunting their wealth in music videos. The *Real Housewives* TV franchise promoted and praised conspicuous consumption. Today, celebrities take to social media to show off their mansions, cars, and vacations.

The more we realize what we lack, the more covetous we feel. Eventually, we can't stand it anymore, so we go into debt to acquire the things we desire. Then the credit card bill arrives—and with it a whole new level of anxiety. Americans are notorious for "spending money we don't have for the things we don't need, to impress people we don't like."

A close cousin of covetousness is envy—the emotion we feel toward another person who has something we lack. We long for their possessions, their looks, their lifestyle, or their social standing. *She's got it. I don't, so I hate her.*

Screens are envy factories. They introduce us to a universe of successful, attractive, pulled-together people who seem to have it all—from the perfectly chiseled male lead to the shapely news anchor with a flawless smile. We gaze at these modern-day gods and goddesses and ask ourselves, "Why don't I look that way?" Eighty-eight percent of women compare their bodies to the images they see in the media, as do 65 percent of men.[10]

We may envy actors and models from afar, but the knife of jealousy is particularly sharp when applied to those we know. People have always compared themselves to others within their social circles. And never has that circle been so large, thanks to social media. Not only are we keeping up with the Joneses, but we're also competing with hundreds or even thousands of acquaintances online.

Image-crafting promotes envy. Social media is like a sports highlight reel: we post our home runs, not our strikeouts. Dallas Hartwig writes, "[O]ur social media feeds read like a modern-day fairy tale, where every moment is wondrous, every interaction with our family is more precious than the last, and even the mundane (coffee with the girls! look at my lunch! stuck in traffic!) is a magical experience."[11]

Seeing our friends' perfectly curated lives on social media can trigger feelings of envy. As we scroll through image after image of acquaintances having amazing experiences, we ask ourselves, *Why isn't my life as great as everyone else's? She's skiing in the Swiss Alps while I'm vacuuming up Cheerios from between the sofa cushions.*

Women seem particularly susceptible to social comparison, in part because they're on social media more. Women are more likely than men to use platforms such as Facebook and Instagram. They are three times more likely to use Pinterest.[12] Women place 55 percent more posts on their Facebook walls than men[13] and take way more "selfies" (photos of themselves).[14]

And speaking of selfies, just 5 percent of women and 16 percent of men post the first headshot they take. Most people shoot anywhere from two to twenty-five selfies before they get a winner. They spend as many as twenty minutes tweaking their selfies with apps such as Facetune to smooth their complexions and make themselves look perfect. People post these idealized images of themselves to social media and wait. If their photo gets a lot of "likes," they feel affirmed. If not, they can become depressed. Over half of respondents said they need more than twenty "likes" to feel good about a selfie.

Psychologist Rachel Andrew describes a recent outbreak of envy among her female patients who can't achieve the lifestyles they see others celebrating on social media. Dr. Andrew sees a pattern: Women begin following social media influencers. They're looking for fashion and beauty tips or home decorating ideas. But the more they watch these YouTube starlets flouting their lustrous hair, trendy outfits, and exquisitely decorated homes, the more envious they become.[15]

The "mean girls" phenomenon predates Facebook by centuries, but social shunning is easier than ever thanks to social media. For example, Charlene logs on to Instagram and sees photos of her friends enjoying themselves at a party. *Why wasn't I invited?* Charlene asks herself. *Perhaps it was just an oversight. Or maybe I'm being shunned.* Either way, Charlene feels publicly humiliated.

Young people sometimes feel envious of the amateur performers they see on video-sharing sites. There are regular teens and young adults who've become overnight sensations by doing something clever in front of a camera and collecting thousands of followers and millions of views. Kids think to themselves, *If he can do it, I can too.* They launch their first video, which gets five views. The next video—seven views. For every successful social media star or influencer, there are legions who've felt the sting of failure.

Video Gaming and Anxiety

The World Health Organization has recognized gaming addiction as a mental health condition. A report published in the *Journal of Health Psychology* studied data from more than 130,000 video game players. Depression and anxiety were particularly prominent among habitual gamers.[16]

How can an activity that's supposed to be relaxing cause so much angst? We've already seen how lean-forward activities overtax the brain. But a lifestyle of heavy gaming also triggers a series of real-life consequences that can lead to anxiety. Before I explain why, let's take a brief look at modern gaming to see who's doing it and what types of games each gender finds captivating.

Both men and women enjoy playing video games, but the sexes differ as to which kinds they prefer. Women are more likely to play on their phones, whereas men comprise the majority of hardcore console and PC gamers. Puzzles, word games, playing-card simulations, and matching games like *Candy Crush* are among women's favorites. Young males prefer war simulations, first-person shooters, and fantasy games that involve frequent combat. Men are the biggest audience for sports simulations (soccer, baseball, basketball, etc.) and sandbox games that allow them to build things, such as *Minecraft*.[17]

A 2017 study from Pew Research Center found that boys and young men make up a disproportionately large share of people who play video games in the United States. Seventy-two percent of men under thirty say they play video games sometimes or often, compared to 49 percent of women in the same age group. As they enter their thirties and forties, the gender gap closes somewhat: men's gaming drops off, but women's remains steady (58 percent versus 48 percent).[18] A third of young men identify themselves as gamers, compared to just 9 percent of young women. Ninety-seven percent of teen boys play video games, compared to 83 percent of girls. Two-thirds of young men ages eighteen to twenty-nine own a gaming console, compared to just 46 percent of women in the same age range.[19]

The most addictive category of games is known as massive multiplayer online role-playing games (MMORPGs). Massive—as in thousands of players around the globe competing and teaming up with each other. Each participant creates a character. The goal of the game is to develop the character's strength and experience, usually through combat. The most popular MMORPGs are based on fantasy themes: dragons, elves, wizards, etc.

To hardcore gamers, MMORPGs are more than a pastime; they're a community. Players organize themselves into clans or guilds, strategizing and talking with each other over headsets. Over time, players become buddies, which cements their commitment to the game. To step away means abandoning your friends.

There's big money in gaming. In 2019, gaming industry revenues were more than three times larger[20] than Hollywood's domestic movie box office receipts.[21] Top-tier gamers can win hundreds of thousands of dollars competing in esports (electronic sports) competitions. These high-stakes tournaments have been broadcast live over the internet and on second-tier cable sports networks since the mid 2010s. When live sports disappeared in response to COVID-19, e-sports helped fill the void. Fox Sports Network, TSN, and ESPN aired e-sports tournaments to cater to an audience hungry for any kind of athletic competition.

Competitive video gaming is now a high school varsity sport in several states, including Connecticut, Georgia, and Kentucky. More than eighty colleges have esports teams, and a few are beginning to award gaming scholarships. In response, some parents are shelling out hundreds of dollars to coaches—that's right, *video game coaches*—to help their kids improve their skills. When your son tells you that he wants to play video games for a living, well, that's a thing.

Now get this: Each day, millions of people log on to their screens not to play video games, but to watch *other* people play video games. Platforms like Twitch, YouTube, and Facebook allow top-tier gamers to broadcast their matches to online audiences numbering in the thousands. These super competitors wear headsets and offer running commentary, sharing game-winning strategies as they wield imaginary weapons. Warning: most of these chats are R- or even X-rated, with plenty of vulgarity and laddish boasting.

Video games promise to become even more addictive as virtual reality (VR) and augmented reality (AR) technologies mature. VR places the gamer into a 3D-simulated world via headset or goggles, while AR games (such as *Pokémon Go*) overlay game content atop the real world. Each day we inch closer to the Matrix.

So why does hardcore gaming create depression and anxiety? Here are some theories:

- In a real-world competition such as a chess tournament, a game of cornhole, or a pick-up basketball game, you compete against a handful of others whose skill levels may be roughly comparable to your own. But in a MMORPG, you're competing against thousands, many of whom are WAY better than you. Gamers may think to themselves, *I'll never be as good as Mr. High Score.*

- Since the competition is so fierce, gamers must spend an enormous amount of time in the game to succeed. That takes a toll on their real lives. Their screen-life victories stand in contrast to real-life failures.

- Men may even compare themselves to their on-screen characters. A gamer may be a muscle-bound champion in the screen world, but a flabby, out-of-shape weakling in the real world. "In my game, I'm a total baller," says sixteen-year-old Mark. "But in school, I'm a nobody." Is it any wonder millions of young men prefer the screen world over the real world?

2.8

How Screens Divide Us into Warring Tribes

Content providers must constantly stock their programs, websites, publications, and social media feeds with wolves to make viewers curious enough to keep coming back. Fear is a dependable wolf. But outrage and contempt are even stronger draws. Nothing makes us feel better about ourselves than looking down on someone else.

And it's never been easier to find someone to look down upon. Our screens serve us a daily all-you-can-sneer-at buffet of corrupt politicians, greedy executives, homicidal soldiers, pedophile priests, incompetent doctors, brutal police, and sanctimonious celebrities. Social media and comment sections provide us with the ideal balcony from which to hurl rotten tomatoes at these hypocrites. We gather with like-minded people and applaud one another with likes and upvotes, glorying in our disdain for the other side.

As we consume story after story of how our leaders have failed us, our trust in them plummets to an all-time low. The media rarely report on the good things our institutions do for us because scandal produces

higher ratings. Why report good news when bad news generates so
many more clicks and pageviews?

All this institution-bashing has led to a decline in civic life. Political scientist Robert Putnam documented how social bonds have been
fraying since the 1950s in his groundbreaking book *Bowling Alone*.
Americans are less politically involved, serve on fewer committees,
and are less likely to join clubs, unions, churches, and PTAs. They
volunteer less often, and membership in fraternal and service organizations such as Rotary, Elks, Shriners, and Kiwanis has fallen apace.
Bowling leagues, women's clubs, and chambers of commerce have also
seen steep declines in participation.

Without regular face-to-face gatherings, people are coming to
trust each other less and less. In fact, the younger generation is the
most distrustful ever polled, according to a Pew Research Center
survey. From the report:

> Around three-quarters (73 percent) of U.S. adults under
> thirty believe people "just look out for themselves" most
> of the time. A similar share (71 percent) say most people
> "would try to take advantage of you if they got a chance,"
> and six in ten say most people "can't be trusted."
>
> All told, nearly half of young adults (46 percent) are
> what the Center's report defines as "low trusters"—people
> who, compared with other Americans, are more likely to
> see others as selfish, exploitative, and untrustworthy, rather
> than helpful, fair, and trustworthy. Older Americans are
> less likely to be low trusters. For example, just 19 percent
> of adults ages sixty-five and older fall into this category,
> according to the survey, which was conducted in late 2018
> among 10,618 U.S. adults.
>
> Young adults also express less confidence in their fellow
> citizens to act in certain civically minded ways. Only

around a third of young Americans (35 percent) say they have a great deal or fair amount of confidence in the American people to respect the rights of those who are not like them—about half the share of adults sixty-five and older who say this (67 percent).[1]

The survey also revealed that millennials were less trustful of the military, clergymen, police officers, and business leaders. The only group in society that young adults trusted more than their older counterparts was college professors.

Millennials are not alone. Gallup found that Americans of all ages put less faith in institutions. The average confidence expressed in seven key institutions declined from 44 percent in 1973 to just 27 percent in 2019. (These are organized religion, public schools, the Supreme Court, Congress, newspapers, organized labor, and big business).[2] These institutions are no more corrupt than they've ever been, but the twenty-four-hour news cycle has magnified their every failure. As our confidence in institutions falls, our contempt for them rises, as does fatalism and cynicism in general. Social media is rampant with comments like these:

Why even vote? Every politician is a dishonest crook.

The system is rigged. Why even try?

Rich people got that way by cheating the little guy.

Why get married? She'll take you to the cleaners in divorce court.

Organized religion is a bunch of hypocrites sticking their noses into other people's business.

So if we've lost faith in established institutions and believe others are out to get us, where do we find groups we can trust? The internet, of course. Social media and online affinity groups allow birds of a feather to flock together as never before. That's a cause for both celebration and concern.

Whether you're a stamp collector, a quilter, or a motorcycle aficionado, there's a group waiting for you to join online. Screen-based groups allow us to connect with people near and far who share our passions. Social media has been credited with facilitating people-power uprisings all over the world, including the Arab Spring, the "Yellow Vest" protests in France, and the Hong Kong demonstrations, to name a few.

But there's a dark side to all this coming together online: as people find their tribes, they become susceptible to *tribalism*. The web not only helps us discover allies; it also helps us identify and attack enemies.

Algorithms: The Cyberworld's Great Dividers

Algorithms begin sorting us the moment we go online. Here's how it works: Websites use "cookies" to keep a record of what we post, click on, and like. As we make our choices, a profile emerges. The algorithm compares our profile with millions of other profiles. Then the algorithm begins serving us content it thinks we will enjoy based on what we and other people like us have chosen to watch, read, like, and click on.

For example, if you like the "I ♥ Siamese Cats" Facebook group, the algorithms begin filling your news feed with delightful videos of furry friends doing adorable things. As you click on the posts you like, the algorithms begin fine-tuning the types of kitty content you receive. One day, you see a sponsored post in your news feed from a local cat shelter asking for volunteers. You sign up, and soon you're a regular at the shelter and are making lots of friends—both feline and human.

In this case, the algorithms provided a valuable service. They helped you find a tribe and enriched your life. You win, and the kitties win.

But Facebook also wins. Once the algorithm identifies you as an ailurophile, advertisers can target you with ads for cat food, feline toys, and local veterinarians. Other cat-oriented groups can pay to have their posts show up in your feed.

On one level, this is magnificent technology. Your screen fills with content you've expressed interest in rather than stuff you don't care about. It's the most efficient advertising technology ever devised: sponsors can zero in on people who are already attracted to their goods and services rather than wasting money on reaching people who aren't.

But the same algorithms that sort us into markets also divide us into ideological tribes. If we "like" someone's posts, algorithms make sure we see more of them. If we comment or interact within a group, that group shows up more often in our feed. Over time, your screen becomes a bias-confirmation machine, buttressing ideas that you are likely to agree with while eliminating anything that might challenge what you already believe.

For the most part, this is unintentional. Facebook and Twitter want us all to get along. But sorting is what algorithms do. On top of this, people have a tendency to banish (unfriend) people who don't share their views, making their feeds even more homogenous. Journalist and filmmaker Jon Ronson said, "Twitter is basically a mutual approval machine. We surround ourselves with people who feel the same way we do, and we approve of each another, and that's really a good feeling. And if somebody gets in the way we screen them out."[3]

This is how our digital kingdom begins taking shape. As I said in the fifth parable, algorithms are the "Yes-Men" that create an online world tailored to our wants, needs, and desires. A conservative man's news feed looks very different from a liberal woman's because algorithms push us toward people and ideas that reinforce our existing worldviews.

However, if you're the type who likes to argue on social media, your feed may fill up with posts, people, and opinions you find disagreeable. The algorithms are watching as you trade punches with ideological foes. The more you spar with these adversaries, the more they show up in your feed. Instead of an echo chamber, your social media becomes a boxing ring.

Screens allow people with fringe points of view to cluster. Type the word *otherkin* into any search box on the web or social media. You'll discover online groups for people who believe themselves to be animals, faeries, wizards, and vampires.

Take the strange case of Eva Tiamat Medusa, who was born a man, claimed to be a woman, and is now identifying as a "Dragon Lady." He's spent some sixty thousand dollars on surgeries to have his earlobes removed, teeth knocked out, nose flattened, and tongue forked. To top it off (literally), he had fake horns implanted on his forehead. Twenty years ago, a person who identified as "trans-species" would have stood alone, but thanks to web search functions and social media, the Dragon Lady found a tribe online that affirms his fantasies and contributes money to his plastic surgery fund.

So the internet allows eccentric people to find each other. What's the harm in that, you ask? Perhaps none. But the web also fuels crazy ideas. Conspiracy theories and misinformation are rampant on the web—and some of them are planted to deliberately sow division and undermine our democracy.

Before the internet, if you held far-left or far-right viewpoints, your main source of news would have been a monthly subscription to *The American Socialist Magazine* or *The John Birch Society Newsletter*. Once every thirty days, a printed publication would appear in your mailbox, filled with essays that buttressed your beliefs. The other twenty-nine days of the month you would be exposed to more moderate news and opinion. But with the internet, extremists can have their worldviews repeatedly confirmed 24/7 by a growing stable of right- and left-leaning outlets. The explosion of far-left and far-right news outlets is hollowing out the political middle in the developed world.

In 1982, CNN launched a show called *Crossfire* that became the template for modern cable news. *Crossfire* featured four political pundits (two liberals versus two conservatives) who argued about the news of the day. This left-versus-right format eventually gave birth to two competing U.S. networks: Fox News Channel began offering news and commentary from a right-wing perspective while MSNBC targeted the left. These two channels skew their news coverage to please their most partisan viewers while gleefully mocking those on the other side.

The web amplified this effect. Site operators learned that sensational headlines stoked fear and outrage—which generated more shares, boosted traffic, and increased ad sales. "Clickbait" was born. Foreign governments such as Russia and Iran were watching, and now they've launched propaganda websites and targeted social media to proliferate misinformation, sow division, and cultivate suspicion among the U.S. populace. Darren Linvill and Patrick Warren spent two years investigating Russian troll factories. They published their findings in *Rolling Stone*:

> Disinformation operations aren't typically fake news or outright lies. Disinformation is most often simply spin. Spin is hard to spot and easy to believe, especially if you are already inclined to do so.
>
> In fall 2018, for example, a Russian account we identified called @PoliteMelanie re-crafted an old urban legend, tweeting: "My cousin is studying sociology in university. Last week she and her classmates polled over 1,000 conservative Christians. 'What would you do if you discovered that your child was a homo sapiens?' 55 percent said they would disown them and force them to leave their home." This tweet, which suggested conservative Christians are not only homophobic but also ignorant, was subtle enough to not feel overtly hateful, but was also aimed directly at multiple cultural stress points, driving a wedge at the point where religiosity and ideology meet. The tweet was

also wildly successful, receiving more than 90,000 retweets and nearly 300,000 likes.

Consistent with past Russian activity, they attacked moderate politicians as a method of bolstering more polarizing candidates...Russia's goals are to further widen existing divisions in the American public and decrease our faith and trust in institutions that help maintain a strong democracy.[4]

Russian trolls have also spread misinformation about vaccine safety to keep frightened parents from inoculating their children. They're trying to slow the rollout of new wireless technology in the West by posting articles falsely linking it to cancer, autism, Alzheimer's, and a host of other illnesses. Troll farms have posted thousands of memes and false news articles "championing veterans and denigrating liberals and minorities."[5] Their goals are transparent: to put Americans' health at risk, dent the West's technological superiority, and make us contemptuous of one another. And it's working. Americans have never been more divided politically. Thomas B. Edsall writes in the *New York Times*:

Just over 42 percent of the people in each party view the opposition as "downright evil." In real numbers, this suggests that 48.8 million voters out of the 136.7 million who cast ballots in 2016 believe that members of opposition party are in league with the devil.[6]

Edsall was quoting a 2019 survey that also found:

• Nearly one out of five Republicans and Democrats agree with the statement that their political adversaries "lack the traits to be considered fully human—they behave like animals."

- Twenty percent of Democrats and 16 percent of Republicans occasionally think the country would be better off if large numbers of the opposition died.
- Eighteen percent of Democrats and 14 percent of Republicans said violence would be justified if the opposing party were to win the next election.
- The most politically active and informed voters were the likeliest to hold these extreme views.

The web has plenty of unwitting amateur trolls too. I have a number of gullible friends and relatives who unknowingly spread misinformation by reposting clickbait articles that are obviously untrue, biased, or exaggerated. I used to try to correct their falsehood-mongering, but it's hard to change the mind of a true believer.

The internet is like rocket fuel for conspiracy theories. Anyone can post a simple blog or create a persuasive meme with misinformation that sounds like it could be true. People who are prone to suspicion share these on their social media pages. The more these falsehoods are shared, the more credible they seem to be.

I've been editing videos since the 1980s, and it's never been easier to reassemble a person's words in a different order than they were originally spoken, making it sound as if they said something they didn't. But an emerging technology takes this to the next level: "Deep-Fake" software can produce realistic-looking videos of people making statements they would never say. It's the ultimate fake news.

Phony profiles have become a huge problem on social media. Automated "bots" harvest photos of real people, set up shadow accounts in their names, and then use these profiles to influence their friends' political views, damage reputations, or ask for money. Facebook shut down more than five billion fake accounts in 2019 alone.[7]

Social media also has a way of amplifying the most strident voices while quieting those in the middle. Extremists aren't shy about sharing their opinions because they believe so passionately in their causes. "Who cares if I come across as pushy?" they say to themselves. "THE FUTURE OF HUMANITY IS AT STAKE!!!" People who hold more moderate, nuanced views often draw fire from the true believers on both right and left, so they keep their opinions to themselves.

All this pressure to join a side is tribalizing us. And the easiest way to prove loyalty to our tribe is by mocking the other side. According to Jonathan Rauch, a senior fellow at the Brookings Institution:

> It turns out that human beings are not wired to be logical creatures that pursue objective truth. We're wired to be tribal creatures that try and ingratiate ourselves with our group and improve our status within that group. The way we do that is displaying outrage, anger, and hostility to the other group.[8]

BBC technology reporter Jane Wakefield writes, "The internet acts like a kind of digital-fueled alcohol, freeing us to say things to strangers that we would never dare to say if we met them."[9] Many comment sections and chat forums allow people to assume screen names and avatars that hide their true identities. Anonymity gives them license to savage one another online, using vicious language they would never use face to face. There's even a name for this: "Online Disinhibition Effect." Psychologist John Suler coined the term "to describe the tendency for people to be more forward, taunting, mean, or aggressive when interacting online as opposed to in person, an effect that was amplified if the poster was anonymous."[10] People tend to be more polite and restrained in person, and studies have shown that eye contact makes them more empathetic to one another. Communicating via screen weakens this empathetic response.

More in Common...

One of the great triumphs of first-world democracies has been the defeat of tribalism. Members of tribal societies sort themselves by religion, family, or clan, which then fight each other for dominance. Corruption flourishes as tribal members steer resources away from the common good and toward the members of their own tribes. Western governments have struggled to bring democracy to places like Afghanistan, Somalia, and Iraq, where tribalism, cronyism, and graft are deeply embedded in the culture.

The citizens of Western democracies have their differences, but they have largely put these aside to unite under a single national identity. However, that hard-fought unity may be unraveling as more and more people segregate themselves by ideology, thanks to their screens.

In 2018, the organization More in Common released a groundbreaking survey of Americans' attitudes toward each other called "Hidden Tribes." The authors wrote:

> In the era of social media and partisan news outlets, America's differences have become dangerously tribal, fueled by a culture of outrage and taking offense. For the combatants, the other side can no longer be tolerated, and no price is too high to defeat them.[11]

But the report also found that 77 percent of Americans believe our differences are not so great that we cannot come together. Two-thirds of Americans are what the report calls "The Exhausted Majority," who are ideologically flexible but not necessarily political centrists. These fair-minded moderates, liberals, and conservatives are tired of the acrimony and are ready to reach across the ideological divide to find common ground. Let's hope it's not too late.

2.9

How Screens Are Changing Communication

Jake and Rebecca are on their first date. They're seated in a bistro, and the waiter has just taken their orders. Jake looks into his date's shimmering brown eyes. He asks a question. Rebecca smiles and replies. And so it goes for the next two hours. She speaks. He replies. He laughs. She blushes. She turns the conversation to another topic. He teases. She feigns surprise.

Around the corner from the bistro, the city council is meeting. The mayor and council members are debating a trio of proposed ordinances. They hear testimony from members of the public. The council votes in favor of two ordinances and rejects the third. Reporters interview the mayor after the meeting adjourns. All of these interactions involve people speaking to one another in real time.

And down the street, Karen sits in her friend Meghan's living room, crying. She's having marriage troubles. Karen speaks. Meghan nods her head, and tears form in the corners of her eyes. They touch hands. They share words for over an hour, experiencing the intense joy of a soul-level connection.

These are but three examples of interpersonal communication. Ever since mankind uttered the first intelligible word, almost all interpersonal communication has taken place face-to-face (F2F). Words were spoken. Emotions were conveyed via tone, facial expression, and body posture. As soon as they were spoken, the words were gone, disappearing into the ether.

About five thousand years ago, the invention of written language changed communication forever. For the first time, words could be *mediated*—captured and preserved by a *medium*, such as clay tablets or paper. But since most people could neither read nor write, spoken words remained the dominant form of interpersonal communication well into the twentieth century.[1] Even into the 1990s, real-time conversation (F2F or via telephone) was the predominant way humans communicated.

Then sometime in the early years of the twenty-first century, humanity crossed a threshold: the majority of interpersonal communication became *screen-mediated*. We began messaging more than we talked. Today, the vast majority of what we say to each other is conveyed via screen. It is written, not spoken—permanently recorded and time-delayed. This shift is not only changing the way we communicate, but also the way we work, think, congregate, and love.

The Importance of F2F

The ability to speak face-to-face in real time is one of the most fundamental human skills. It means the difference between success and failure in life. Every relationship, business transaction, and social movement depends on people who can appropriately convey their ideas, opinions, and emotions through words, facial expressions, and body language. These so-called "soft skills" are often more important than physical prowess or technical know-how.

How do we learn to converse? By having conversations—hundreds of thousands of them over the course of a lifetime. We begin by speaking to our parents and siblings and then to our teachers and classmates. Our communication skills blossom through social gatherings, workplace collaboration, argumentation, and casual chats with strangers.

Yet this ancient practice may be withering in our generation. Teachers, employers, and counselors are noticing a growing number of young adults who are very uncomfortable with F2F conversation. Talking to another person in real time feels awkward. Instead, they prefer screen-mediated communication: texts, emails, direct messages, and social media posts.

According to a study from Pew Research Center, a third of adults prefer texting over all other forms of communication (including F2F).[2] Among eighteen- to twenty-two-year-olds, 77 percent prefer texting. Texting is the most-used form of communication among adults under age fifty.

Many young adults assume screen-mediated communication has been around a long time, but until the mid-1990s, these tools were used mainly by computer geeks. Note how recently the breakthroughs in screen-mediated communication have appeared:

- 1978—first computer bulletin board service (BBS) allows posting of messages
- 1980—first computer chat room to offer real-time communication
- 1991—World Wide Web comes online and first website goes live
- 1993—first phone-to-phone text message sent
- 1996—first free email service offered (Hotmail)
- 1997—first social media platform launches (Six Degrees)
- 1997—first instant messaging service goes live (AOL)
- 1999—text messages can be shared between mobile networks

Let's stop here. Prior to 1999, the world still communicated primarily in real time (F2F and by phone). Person #1 said something, and person #2 heard it.

But in the space of a generation, the vast majority of interpersonal communication went from being delivered mouth-to-ear to being delivered screen-to-eye. Instead of disappearing, every word is now recorded and time-delayed by our screens. This places an additional burden on the communicator to craft the perfect message.

Let's go back to the bistro with Jake and Rebecca. She smiles and asks Jake a question. How long does Jake have to craft a response? Perhaps three seconds at the most? There's no time to think or edit. Jake must say something, or there's an uncomfortable silence that can ruin the date.

But after the date, Rebecca sends Jake a text. Now how long does Jake have to reply? As much time as he needs. Thirty seconds, five minutes, or all night if he wants. If he's not fond of Rebecca, he can simply "ghost" her by choosing not to reply at all.

This is what I mean by *time-delayed*. Since Jake has time to think about what he texts (and Rebecca knows it), he's under subtle pressure to craft the perfect rejoinder. How many times have you agonized over a text message, deleting and rewriting it two or three times to get it just right?

But even more perilous is the fact that everything we say via screen leaves a permanent record—a time-bomb that can blow up on us later. This forces us to approach every email, text, and social media post with a higher level of care than we would a simple conversation.

Spoken words can be misinterpreted, but screen-mediation can cause the smallest misunderstanding to erupt. How many times have you sent a message or posted something to social media, trying to be funny or ironic, but your recipient took it the wrong way? That's because words on a screen can't convey the rich bouquet of emotions that F2F can. Studies have shown that eye contact, facial expressions, and body language communicate as much or more than the words we say. Emojis can help, but even those can be misconstrued.

Screen-mediated conversation is fine when it supplements a rich F2F relationship. But when it replaces F2F, the result is loneliness and isolation. Dr. Zack Carter asks, "Are you hiding behind your texts?":

> [T]exting delivers an illusion of intimacy, providing people the often favorable opportunity to limit emotional disclosure to text and emojis on a screen, dodge conflict, and evade relational connection, maintenance, and growth. When used properly, texting is advised to be used to compliment face-to-face relationships, instead of supersede or replace [them].[3]

Screen-based novelty and screen-mediated communication are very new to the human experience. Our brains will eventually adapt. But in the meantime, real-time F2F conversation skills remain vitally important to success in life and relationships, which is the subject of our next chapter.

2.10

Swipe Left:
How Screens Are
Weakening Relationships

Picture a farmer walking behind a plow, tearing up virgin land. He's disturbing a complex ecosystem of grasses and plants that developed over centuries. A sower follows with seeds that will grow into exotic new crops the land has never before produced.

This is what screens are doing to interpersonal relationships—plowing up centuries of painstakingly developed social customs and replacing them with completely new ways of relating. Our screens, novelty factories that they are, discourage the traditional and promote the trendy. The media encourage us to plow up the oppressive relational boundaries our ancestors recognized and to live according to our own feelings. In return, we're promised an abundant crop of fulfillment and autonomy.

So how is our crop doing? Since the dawn of the screen age, rates of family dissolution and single parenthood have risen dramatically. Depression and suicide are near historic levels. The share of U.S. adults who live alone has has (bc of since)nearly doubled since the 1950s, and one in four children lives in a fatherless home.[1] The Health Resources and Services

117

Administration says the United States is in the throes of a "loneliness epidemic." Screens offer us a level of interconnection never before possible, yet we've never felt lonelier. We sowed the seeds of personal autonomy, but we have reaped a harvest of isolation.

Loneliness is particularly acute among the young. A George Mason University study found that one-third of youths under age twenty-five felt lonely, while only 11 percent of adults over sixty-five felt the same. Another study in the U.K. found similar results: 40 percent of sixteen- to twenty-four-year-olds often felt lonely, compared to 27 percent of adults over seventy-five.[2] A YouGov poll found that 27 percent of millennials say they have no close friends, and 22 percent claim to have no friends at all. To compare, just 9 percent of Baby Boomers are similarly friendless.[3] And the young adults who use social media most frequently—fifty or more times in a typical week—were three times more likely to perceive themselves as socially isolated than those who go online fewer than nine times a week.[4]

This increase in loneliness has led to a dramatic rise in depression and suicidal ideation, especially among girls:

> Between 2009 and 2017, rates of depression among kids ages 14 to 17 increased by more than 60 percent, the study found. The increases were nearly as steep among those ages 12 to 13 (47 percent) and 18 to 21 (46 percent), and rates roughly doubled among those ages 20 to 21.
>
> Among young people, rates of suicidal thoughts, plans and attempts all increased significantly, and in some cases more than doubled, between 2008 and 2017, the study found.[5]

Depression doesn't rise 60 percent in less than a decade for no reason, nor do suicide rates suddenly double without a cause. So what changed between 2009 and 2017? We started carrying screens around with us 24/7.

Dunbar's Number

Robin Dunbar is an anthropologist at the University of Oxford. After studying how people formed groups throughout history and across cultures, Dunbar reached a startling conclusion: human brain capacity places upper limits on the number of relationships one person can manage:

- 1,500 people you recognize
- 500 acquaintances
- 150 meaningful contacts
- 50 friends
- 15 good friends
- 5 loved ones

These numbers, of course, are averages. Extreme extroverts can maintain a larger circle, while introverts might faint if asked to identify fifteen good friends. But across time and cultures, Dunbar's formula is surprisingly accurate.

Let's look at Dunbar's principle another way using fuel as a metaphor. Let's say each of us has ten liters of "relationship fuel" to expend. In the days before social media, we used our fuel this way:

- Five liters to maintain our close face-to-face relationships
- Two liters establishing new friendships
- One liter building and maintaining professional relationships
- One liter staying in touch with distant relatives

- One liter to old friends and keeping up with far-flung acquaintances

In the old days, there was no easy way to keep up with high school buddies, past business acquaintances, and second cousins once removed. So we invested most of our friendship fuel on the people we saw frequently.

But now, thanks to social media, we can stay connected to people we used to know. On one level, this is a wonderful privilege. There's nothing wrong with staying in touch.

But if we invest seven or eight liters of relationship fuel on people we rarely see in person, we may lack the fuel to maintain and build relationships with the people we are with often. We end up with a ton of old friends, but few current or new ones.

I see this all the time: the man who has no friends except for buddies he keeps up with online from "the good old days," the young adult who goes off to college but has trouble making friends because she brought her social network from home along, and the parent who's popular on social media but barely knows his own kids.

Screen-mediated relationships are often shallow and based on sharing trivia. I know lots of young adults whose entire online discourse consists of posting silly memes and making fun of things: failed institutions, bad ideas, and—of course—people who think differently. They have hundreds of people to joke with but nobody to get deep with. Hence, they feel alone.

Screens may be eroding our relational grit—that is, our ability to stay friends with people who annoy us, offend us, or mildly hurt us. Why should a person put up with a real-life friend who bugs her when she's got 1,900 friends she can hold at arm's length on Facebook?

The net effect of all this screen-mediated friending is real-life loneliness. And no generation is lonelier than the current crop of young adults. Theirs was once the sociable generation, assembling in public spaces, doing things with friends, and going out on dates with the opposite sex.

How Screens Are Distorting the Dating Scene

Remember dating? You sometimes see it portrayed in classic movies. A gentleman asks a lady to accompany him to dinner, a movie, a stage play, or a concert. They dress up. They exchange clever banter. They smile a lot. The evening ends with a moonlit walk and a passionate kiss. Dating was so ... romantic.

Dating as we know it hasn't been around very long. For most of human history, girls were married off around puberty, often to older men who had the financial means to support them. Even into the nineteenth century, the majority of marriages continued to be arranged by parents and matchmakers. Courting finally became widespread during the Victorian era, but the marriage market was limited to people who ran in the same social circles. The modern dating scene arrived during the roaring 1920s as couples began meeting at work, parties, nightclubs, and social events.

But then the machines got involved. Dating and mating would never be the same.

Computers began expanding the U.S. dating pool in 1965 when two Harvard University students opened "Operation Match." Singles filled out a paper questionnaire, which they mailed in with a three-dollar fee. Each single's data was fed into a computer that spat out punch cards representing compatible men and women based on personality traits. Seven to fourteen days later, a list of "matches" arrived in the mail.[6]

Thirty years later, Match.com launched as the first online dating service, allowing singles to find one another from the comfort of their home PCs. Suddenly, daters could peruse hundreds of online profiles complete with headshots for one monthly fee. Users could sort potential sweethearts by age, gender, location, hobbies, lifestyle—and most importantly, looks. Various online romance portals sprang up, ranging from marriage-focused platforms like eHarmony and Christian Mingle to infidelity sites like Ashley Madison, which is marketed under the slogan "Life is short. Have an affair."

In 2009, the first mobile dating app launched. Called Grindr, it featured geolocation, which allowed gay men (its target audience) to see a map of potential sex partners. Grindr for straight people launched in 2012. Dubbed Tinder, the app presents men and women with an all-you-can-swipe buffet of potential mates, dates, and hookups. No need to go to a bar or dress for a party. Singles can view and pursue hundreds of potential lovers within a user-specified geographic radius. Tinder claims to have produced more than thirty billion matches in its first decade.

Although Tinder has certainly led to some LTRs (long-term relationships), the app is best known as a way to meet people for casual sex. Download the app, link it to your Facebook (to discourage trolls and fakes), upload five pictures and a brief bio, and you're ready to go. Now it's time to start swiping. Swipe left on the people you don't like and swipe right on the ones you do. If you get a match, the two of you can chat and decide whether to meet up. Many Tinder competitors have sprung up, including Bumble, where women make the first move.

This explosion of choice is distorting the dating market. Professor David Buss teaches psychology at the University of Texas. He says dating apps give young adults the impression that there are thousands of potential mates available to them, which causes young men to play the field:

> When there is a surplus of women, or a perceived surplus of women, the whole mating system tends to shift towards short-term dating. Marriages become unstable. Divorces

increase. Men don't have to commit, so they pursue a short-term mating strategy. Men are making that shift, and women are forced to go along with it in order to mate at all.[7]

The stats back this up. In 1960, the average age of first marriage was twenty for women and twenty-two for men. Today, it's twenty-seven and twenty-nine. Thanks to the widespread availability of contraception, casual hookups, and simulated sex such as pornography, men are in much less of a hurry to marry. (You've heard the old saying: Why buy the cow when the milk is free?) Meanwhile, screens continue to expand our romantic options beyond anything humans have ever experienced.

Good-looking people have always found it easier to entice the opposite sex. But dating apps, with their heavy emphasis on an attractive headshot, have greatly magnified the value of physical beauty. Gorgeous women are mobbed online, while handsome, successful alpha males enjoy a virtual harem of "Tinderellas." Nancy Jo Sales quotes a young Wall Street investment banker named Alex in *Vanity Fair*:

> "With these dating apps," he says, "you're always sort of prowling. You could talk to two or three girls at a bar and pick the best one, or you can swipe a couple hundred people a day—the sample size is so much larger. It's setting up two or three Tinder dates a week and, chances are, sleeping with all of them, so you could rack up 100 girls you've slept with in a year."[8]

So that's the Faustian bargain dating apps offer: young, attractive, and successful men gorge on casual sex. Women play along, telling themselves it's better this way: *I don't need a man right now; I need to focus on my career.* Everyone pretends to be having a good time as they exchange emotional intimacy and spiritual oneness for a quick hookup and commitment-free sexual release.

Meanwhile, lower-status or less attractive people struggle to get any attention from the opposite sex. Involuntarily celibate men (incels) meet each other on the internet and blame "sexual inequality" for their relationship woes. Many drown their sorrows in pornography, which just adds to their isolation and relational despair.

Traditional dating—where a couple gets to know each other before removing their clothing—still exists, but even here screens are changing the rules. Once the date begins, beware of:

Phubbing: Short for "phone-snubbing," phubbing occurs when a couple pays more attention to their devices than to each other. Go into any restaurant and you'll see couples phubbing.

Ghosting: After what seemed like a successful date, one party disappears like a ghost.

Cloaking: Extreme ghosting. After a date, one person blocks the other on every social media and dating platform.

Zombieing: Contacting someone you ghosted in the past, acting like nothing's amiss.

Ghosting mid-date: He excuses himself to go to the bathroom and never returns. He then pulls out his phone and begins swiping for another date. What a lizard.

■   ■   ■

Screen-mediated dating isn't all bad. Not everyone who uses a dating app is seeking a sexual bacchanal. I know several couples who have found successful marriages online. But on the whole, screens' impact on love and romance has been negative. The explosion of choice is making people less patient with each other. Relationships are becoming transactional and self-centered. And with so many other potential matches just a finger swipe away, why should a couple stick together when things get rocky? Lauren Weir writes:

Our relationship with our phones has often coddled us, enamored us with our own love of ease, and brainwashed us, creating the false belief that relationships should be as easy as the tap of a screen. The influence of our phones can leave us desiring depth without work, intimacy without long-suffering, and community without commitment.[9]

Unfortunately, I haven't yet mentioned the Number One threat that screens present to relational and sexual intimacy. I'll reveal the ultimate form of unsafe sex in our next chapter.

2.11

Pornography:
The Ultimate Unsafe Sex

**(WARNING: The next two chapters contain
frank descriptions of sexual activity and may be
inappropriate for some readers.)**

What's the big deal with pornography? Sexual desire is natural and healthy. Why shouldn't we indulge ourselves with porn? Anna Pulley writes in Salon:

> Unlike physical sex, watching porn spreads no diseases, leads to zero pregnancies, and doesn't engage with vicious judgments like slut-shaming (unless, you know, you're into that). Plus, using porn to satisfy one's sexual needs is safe, free-to-cheap, and convenient. And it can even be used as a sex aid for [real life] sex, as many couples can attest.[1]

Porn has many defenders, particularly in the comments section of websites. Here's one from a reader who goes by the handle Alex in

SoCal, posted following a *Washington Post* story advising parents to warn their kids about the dangers of porn:

"Actually, watching porn is normal and healthy, just like masturbation is."

No, Alex. Watching strangers performing sex acts is about as abnormal and unhealthy as anything you can imagine. Seeing naked people having sex is something we never witness in real life. On top of this, the brain is strongly attuned to sexual stimulation because humanity's survival depends on sexual desire. These two triggers make internet pornography a powerful wolf—novelty that sinks its teeth in and won't let go. Porn is so overpowering it can actually alter the neural pathways in your brain:

> Repeated consumption of porn causes the brain to literally rewire itself. It triggers the brain to pump out chemicals and form new nerve pathways, leading to profound and lasting changes....[2]

The initial exposure to porn releases a flood of chemicals that overwhelms the brain's reward centers. The brain quickly habituates to this abnormal level of sexual stimulation, which causes the user to seek even more-extreme forms of pornography to achieve the same level of reward. Normal sexual activity can't match the hyperstimulation caused by porn.

For years, religious leaders have sounded the alarm about sexualized screen content. Secularists and progressives dismissed their concerns, accusing them of being old-fashioned, repressed prudes. But as the sexual revolution enters its seventh decade, a growing number of non-religious clinicians, psychologists, and professors are acknowledging the dangers of porn. Secular organizations such as Fight the New Drug and NoFap have emerged to help nonreligious men conquer their porn and masturbation habits.[3] Their goal is not piety, but potency.

Porn: The New Drug

Photographic pornography has existed only since the mid-1800s and was made illegal in the United States beginning in 1873. Vice laws were relaxed after World War II, and Hugh Hefner democratized and upscaled porn with the debut of *Playboy* magazine in December 1953. The first-edition cover was tame by today's standards, featuring Marilyn Monroe in a one-piece bathing suit.

Porn was available when I was a teen growing up in the swinging '70s, but it was relatively hard to get. You had to be eighteen to purchase a "dirty" magazine or see an X-rated movie. Boys of my generation managed to get their hands on a few rumpled copies of *Playboy*, which they passed around or hid under their mattresses. If you didn't care for Miss September, you had to wait thirty days to see Miss October.

Pornography came to life with the introduction of VCRs in the late 1970s. Video-rental stores popped up all over America, many with "Adults Only" sections in the back. These tapes created a generation of VHS voyeurs who lay in bed watching actors perform exotic sex acts on their TVs. About this same time, doctors and psychologists began to see an influx of patients with sexual dysfunction and addiction issues, and video porn was almost always a major contributing factor. A new organization called Sexaholics Anonymous held its first national convention in 1981—five years after the introduction of the VCR.

But even into the 1990s, there were still barriers to porn access. Stores kept dirty magazines behind the counter. Mailing hardcore pornography was illegal, so users had to visit adult bookstores in a seedy part of town. And it was embarrassing to walk up to the video rental counter with a copy of *Debbie Does Dallas*. "What if a neighbor sees?"

Then along came the internet—and every barrier to pornographic viewing fell in the blink of an eye:[4]

Once porn hit the Web in the 1990s, suddenly there was nothing but a few keystrokes between anyone with an internet connection and the most graphic material available.[5] The online porn industry exploded. Between 1998 and 2007, the number of pornographic websites grew by 1,800 percent.[6] By 2004, porn sites were getting three times more visitors than Google, Yahoo!, and MSN Search put together.[7] It was "big business" in a way the world had never seen before. Thirty percent of all internet data was related to porn,[8] and worldwide porn revenues (including internet, sex shops, videos rented in hotel rooms, etc.) grew to exceed the incomes of Microsoft, Google, Amazon, eBay, Yahoo!, Apple, Netflix, and Earthlink combined.[9]

All those billions of dollars caught the attention of broadcast and cable TV, which scrambled to catch up. Between 1998 and 2005, the number of sex scenes on TV nearly doubled.[10] Video game characters became more sexualized as females got bustier while males grew hypermuscular.

In the fantasy world of porn, every man is Hercules while every woman is a lusty vixen desperate for kinky sex. After repeated exposure to these fantasies, our brains come to expect this in the real world. Then real boy meets real girl. They've both seen a lot of porn. She has an imperfect body and a normal libido. Meanwhile, he can't possibly "measure up" to the freaks she sees on the screen. Plus, real people are complex. They have emotional needs. Sometimes he's in the mood, and she isn't. He has a porn-induced fetish she finds disgusting. Over time, some porn users give up on real relationships because screen-based sex simulations are simply easier to manage.

Porn so warps our expectations that we can't negotiate the ups and downs of a real, lasting relationship. Levi Lusko writes:

> You can't spend hundreds of hours looking at thousands and thousands of naked, airbrushed, artificial young bodies, and then expect to be satisfied with one real, imperfect, aging person when you get married. If you are hooked on pornography when you're single, you will bring your addiction into your marriage, and it will rot out your relationship from the inside out.[11]

Porn exalts physical pleasure above all else, crippling the user's ability to love selflessly:

> Studies show that exposure to pornography can lead to a decreased interest in committed relationships and less satisfaction for those who are in one. This is because porn can start to strip away the deeply emotional and selfless connection that intimacy creates, and replace it with self-focused sexual desire. In fact, there are forums all over the internet with people saying that they can't be sexually satisfied without porn.
>
> What about those people who say it's healthy to consume porn with a partner to "spice things up"? The truth is coming out in studies, which show that what really happens is that the consumer ends up trying to imitate what they've seen in porn and comparing their partner to it.
>
> On the surface, porn might seem to provide an immediate spark for excitement and novelty...at least at first. That is exactly what studies presumably showing the "positive effects of porn" on relationships are measuring—initial, surface, self-reported "positives" for relationships.
>
> But what happens to the romance of couples who consume porn long-term? The long-term studies paint a very different picture. The preponderance of evidence from a

dozen or more in-depth, longer-term studies consistently show porn consumption lowering relationship satisfaction, emotional closeness, and sexual satisfaction.[12]

Porn is not only warping minds; it's incapacitating healthy young bodies. Amy Fleming writes in *The Guardian*:

> Viagra's core market used to be older men in poor health, but according to a number of studies and surveys, between 14 percent and 35 percent of young men experience ED [Erectile Dysfunction]. "It's crazy but true," says Mary Sharpe of the Reward Foundation, an educational charity focusing on love, sex, and the internet. "Until 2002, the incidence of men under 40 with ED was around 2-3 percent. Since 2008, when free-streaming, high-definition porn became so readily available, it has steadily risen."[13]

Frequent masturbation is causing men to "release all the pressure behind the dam," so to speak. When it's time to perform with a real woman, there's nothing left. Men in their twenties are getting penile implant operations because they cannot maintain an erection. Amy Fleming continues:

> In online forums dedicated to porn-induced erectile dysfunction (PIED), tens of thousands of young men share their struggles to stop using pornography, their progression from soft porn to hardcore and the barriers they face in forming real-life romantic and sexual relationships. It is hard to prove outright that pornography causes ED, but these testimonies replicate findings from the clinical literature: that if men can kick their porn habit, they start to recover their ability to become aroused by real-life intimacy.

As porn access has exploded on the internet, there's been a race to the bottom as pornographers compete to produce darker, more violent porn:

> "Thirty years ago 'hardcore' pornography usually meant the explicit depiction of sexual intercourse," writes Dr. Norman Doidge, a neuroscientist and author of *The Brain That Changes Itself.* "Now hardcore has evolved and is increasingly dominated by the sadomasochistic themes…all involving scripts fusing sex with hatred and humiliation."[14] In our post-*Playboy* world, porn now features degradation, abuse, and humiliation of people in a way never before seen in the mass media.[15] "[S]oftcore is now what hardcore was a few decades ago," Doidge explains. "The comparatively tame softcore pictures of yesteryear…now show up on mainstream media all day long, in the pornification of everything, including television, rock videos, soap operas, advertisements, and so on."[16]

Why has pornography taken such a dark turn? As porn floods the internet, users are becoming overexposed—and desensitized. The more we see anything (whether it's porn, violence, poverty, or natural disasters), the less our brains react to it. It becomes normal—a tree rather than a wolf. A trio of researchers who analyzed the fifty most popular pornographic films of 2010 wrote:

> Findings indicate high levels of aggression in pornography in both verbal and physical forms. Of the 304 scenes analyzed, 88.2 percent contained physical aggression, principally spanking, gagging, and slapping, while 48.7 percent of scenes contained verbal aggression, primarily name-calling. Perpetrators of aggression were usually male,

whereas targets of aggression were overwhelmingly female. Targets [the women] most often showed pleasure or responded neutrally to the aggression.[17]

Men slapping, choking, and ejaculating in women's faces (that's called a facial) while the women pretend to enjoy it. Don't tell me this isn't affecting how men relate to women in real life.

But even hardcore porn users eventually habituate. They need something new and exciting. And that's where things can go off the rails. I call this the *porn-to-predator pipeline*:

- First exposure to porn
- Becomes a habitual porn user
- Brain becomes desensitized
- Seeks out ever more extreme, bizarre, and sadistic forms of pornography
- Crosses the line into illegal child porn
- Begins chatting online with children
- Tries to meet and have sex with children

Now, I need to stop and make something very clear: not every person who uses porn crosses the line. However, porn fuels every child predator's descent into darkness. Those who swim with jellyfish will eventually be stung.

If you still think porn doesn't hurt anybody, consider this: Children as young as six years old are sexually assaulting one another. Where could they possibly have learned these things? Sam Black writes:

Children influenced by pornography are sexually assaulting other children, said Heidi Olson, a sexual assault nurse examiner who works with children only. This isn't older teens having sex. No, she describes 6-to-10-year-olds acting out adult sexual behaviors, and they are mimicking what they see in pornography.

"We are seeing a rise of perpetrators who have no risk factors except for exposure to pornography," said Olson of Children's Mercy Hospital in Kansas City, MO. "Pornography is influencing children to sexually act out, assault, and hurt their peers like we've never seen."

Olson and other professionals are seeing a direct correlation between early exposure to pornography and children mimicking adult sexual behaviors and sexually assaulting (including raping) other children. Of the 1,000 children who reported their sexual abuse to the hospital in 2017, the majority of the victims were girls around 4 to 8 years old.[18]

And finally, how does an empty bank account sound? Porn is a multibillion-dollar business, earning more money in a typical year than Major League Baseball, the National Basketball Association, and the National Football League combined.[19] With so much free pornography available, how does the porn industry generate this mountain of cash?

Pornographers are like fishermen. They put out a lure (free porn) to habituate your mind. Then they wait. Pretty soon the pleasure centers of your brain get bored. Meanwhile, the pornographers keep offering you "premium content," a euphemism for hardcore porn. Desperate for dopamine and longing for sexual release, you type in your credit card number. Just like that, they've caught their fish. And there's a permanent record of your purchase sitting on a server.

Once they have your credit card number, the pornographers hand you off to "cam girls"—women who perform live sex acts over webcams. Your money disappears fast when you're paying for female attention by the minute. Virtual reality is the next frontier in screen sex. Put on a headset and experience lifelike, 3D simulations that respond to your body movements.

There is much more I could say. Sadly, I have twelve more pages of notes on this topic. There seems to be no limit to the obscene ways our screens can be used to violate and subjugate us.

There is no healthy amount of pornography. Studies have shown even a tiny amount of porn use diminishes real-life sexual satisfaction.[20] And every porn user is contributing to an industry that's harming society and degrading to all who participate in it.

Millions are drowning in pornography, but there's always hope of a rescue. Every day, hundreds of men and women leave porn behind forever. I'll be sharing their successful strategies in Section Three of this book.

2.12

Predators' Playground

Roo Powell is a thirty-seven-year-old woman who uses software to assume false online identities.[1] Tonight, she's turning herself into an eleven-year-old girl named Bailey. In the past month, she's posed as fifteen-year-old Libby, sixteen-year-old Kait, and fourteen-year-old Ava.

To complete tonight's deception, Roo swathes her wrists in neon hair ties and splashes her nails with glitter polish. She pulls on a loose-fitting hoodie, looks into a camera, and lets software do the rest. The crows' feet around her eyes disappear, her cheeks become slimmer, and her skin smooths to resemble that of a bright-eyed eleven-year-old girl.

Roo has been impersonating schoolgirls for almost a year with the assistance of four male accomplices. They operate cameras, help with disguises, and record conversations. Their goal: to gather evidence against online predators. Roo runs the Special Projects Team at Bark, a tech company that helps parents monitor their children's online activity.

With the preparation done, it's showtime. Roo uploads a photo to Instagram: a selfie of "Bailey" smiling at the camera. The caption reads, "v excitedd to see my friends this weekend at carly's party! Ilysm!!" Roo types a few emojis for good measure.

She doesn't have to wait long.

In less than a minute, the messages from adult men begin arriving. First one, then two more, and three more. Within two hours, fifteen adult men have contacted Bailey. "Half of them could be charged with transfer of obscene content to a minor," Roo writes. "Nine months of this, and we still continue to be stunned by the breadth of cruelty and perversion we see."

The men begin by flirting with Bailey. They ask for pictures. They pretend to be teenagers, asking to be her boyfriend. They call her "baby," not realizing the irony.

Five minutes after her Instagram post goes out, the first nude video arrives: a man showing himself masturbating. Moments later, the same man sends a photo of his erect penis. The man asks Bailey for a topless photo. She refuses. He begins to describe oral and vaginal sex to the eleven-year-old, using language that would make a barkeeper blush.

Instagram has a calling feature, and Bailey's virtual "phone" begins ringing. It's an incoming video call from another man. Roo quickly changes costumes and answers. She's greeted by a twenty-something fellow with a British accent, breathing heavily. He's lying in bed, shirtless. He asks Bailey to do the same.

After two-and-a-half hours of this, Roo is exhausted. She has fielded seven video calls (and ignored another two dozen). She's text-chatted with seventeen different men, eleven of whom sent pictures of their genitals.

Roo and her partners spend the rest of the evening cataloging photos, videos, and conversations, packaging them for law enforcement.[2]

Picture an eleven-year-old girl sitting on a park bench. Within minutes, she's surrounded by a mob of adult men exposing themselves and inviting her to have sex using lurid, graphic language to describe their twisted fantasies. Society would be outraged if something like this happened in the real world. We'd summon the police, and the press would give the story wall-to-wall coverage. Yet this sort of abuse goes largely unreported in the screen world. Thousands of girls and boys are introduced to sexual perversion each day via their social media accounts.

It's not just men who are using these platforms to stalk children. Twenty-one-year-old Gemma Watts posed as a sixteen-year-old boy online. She "masculinized" her profile picture and took the name Jake Waton. She "liked" profiles of girls aged thirteen to sixteen and began messaging them, sharing flattering messages and intimate photos (presumably of male bodies). "Jake" eventually met up with several of her victims and groped them repeatedly. She even stuffed socks into her underwear to trick her prey into thinking she was male. Police believe Watts may have duped as many as fifty teen girls, at least two of whom later attempted suicide.[3]

This is going to be a hard chapter to read, but please stay with it. My goal is not to cause panic or disgust you, but to open your eyes to what's really happening online. Take a deep breath as we dive into one of the darkest corners of cyberspace.

We Were Warned

Social media platforms launched in the 2000s with the promise of bringing people together. But our naïve belief in the goodness of humanity blinded us to social media's gravest danger: granting people anonymous, long-distance access to each other.

We had a warning. It was called the telephone.

Prior to Alexander Graham Bell's 1876 invention, all conversation had taken place face to face. The telephone was the first device that allowed people to speak to one another over a long distance. But it also introduced a new feature: *anonymity*. This gave rise to the prank phone call, something I did a few times when I was a kid:

[Phone rings] Homeowner: Hello?

Me: Hi, this is the appliance repairman. Is your refrigerator running?

Homeowner: Yes, it is…

Me: Well, you'd better go catch it. Ha ha ha! *CLICK*.

But this bit of harmless fun had a dark cousin: obscene or threatening phone calls. In the days before Caller ID, it was not unusual to pick up the phone and hear a man breathing heavily on the other end of the line. If a woman answered, the caller might ask, "What are you wearing, baby?" or suggest something sexual to her. If she hung up, he would often call again and again. Victims had few remedies other than to leave the phone off the hook, but that kept legitimate calls from coming through. Since almost everyone's name, number, and home address were printed in the phone book, obscene phone calls were unnerving.

So we've known for more than a century what happens when people can access one another anonymously. The vast majority of people use the technology responsibly, but some abuse it for vile purposes.

Which brings us to social media. Unlike a telephone that restricts the user to one conversation at a time, social media users can reach out to dozens of people simultaneously, multiplying humanity's capacity to do remarkable good—and unspeakable evil.

Sex traffickers are using sophisticated algorithms to target young women via social media, says Gwen Adams, executive director of Priceless, a non-profit that rescues victims of sexual exploitation in Alaska. Traffickers employ software to scan millions of social media profiles, looking for girls from single-parent homes or those who engage in high-risk behaviors. Using fake profiles, traffickers "befriend" these girls on social media and trick them into sending nude photos, which they use to blackmail the girls into prostitution. Some traffickers arrange to meet up with their victims, drug them, and photograph them in compromising positions. The frightened girls often give in to the extortion. They never meet their pimps. The entire scam is executed via screen.

The *New York Times* wrote a stunning exposé titled "The Internet Is Overrun with Images of Child Sexual Abuse. What Went Wrong?"[4] The article begins:

Twenty years ago, the online images were a problem; 10 years ago an epidemic. Now, the crisis is at a breaking point.

The images are horrific. Children, some just 3 or 4 years old, being sexually abused and in some cases tortured. "The predominant sound is the child screaming and crying," according to a federal agent quoted in the documents.

Pictures of child sexual abuse have long been produced and shared to satisfy twisted adult obsessions. But it has never been like this: Technology companies reported a record 45 million online photos and videos of the abuse last year [more than double the number from the previous year, and 400 times more than a decade earlier].

In a particularly disturbing trend, online groups are devoting themselves to sharing images of younger children and more extreme forms of abuse. The groups use encrypted technologies and the dark web, the vast underbelly of the internet, to teach pedophiles how to carry out the crimes and how to record and share images of the abuse worldwide.

Multiple police investigations over the past few years
have broken up enormous dark web forums, including one
known as Child's Play that was reported to have had over
a million user accounts.

Alicia Kozakiewicz was the first widely reported internet-related
child abduction victim.[5] On New Year's Day in 2002, thirteen-year-
old Alicia was kidnapped outside her home after being groomed by a
man who found her online. Her kidnapper chained, raped, and beat
her. He filmed the abuse and streamed it over the internet to a paying
audience. Fortunately, someone who saw the video contacted the FBI.
Alicia was rescued and her abductor was arrested.

Human cruelty isn't new. Recording and selling it to a worldwide
audience is. These videos depict real youngsters in anguish; their
torment is captured and sold for the sick pleasure of others. The
commercialization of sexual abuse and suffering is made possible by
our screens.

Obsessed with Child Safety?

It's ironic: Society has become absolutely fixated on children's
physical safety. Parents have been arrested for letting their
nine-year-olds walk to school or play alone at a neighborhood
park. But a child with an internet-enabled device is far more likely
to be victimized than one who governs herself in a public space.
Predators no longer hide in the bushes. Instead, they prowl social
media, cloaked in anonymity, stalking hundreds of potential victims at once.

Naomi Schaefer Riley has written a book whose subtitle perfectly
captures our upside-down approach to child safety: *Stop Banning
Seesaws and Start Banning Snapchat*. It's time to focus on the real

dangers our children face today—threats that enter not through an unlocked door, but through an unmonitored device.

I'm Ready to Get My Screen Use under Control

3.1

The Parable of the Four Brothers

Now that you understand what screens are doing to society, it's time for a bit of self-reflection. How is screen life affecting you? Your friends and loved ones? Let's begin the discussion with another parable:

> Four brothers lived on a farm. They rose early, worked hard all day, and ate what their flocks and fields produced. All four enjoyed excellent health, thanks to a combination of regular exercise and a balanced diet.
>
> But the farm fell upon hard times and had to be sold. The brothers moved to the city in search of work. There they found the foods they had always enjoyed—and in great abundance. They also discovered delicious but unhealthy foods they'd never experienced in the country.
>
> • The first brother (Moderate Mike) continued to eat sensible portions of healthy foods.

- The second brother (Excessive Eddie) ate healthy foods, but in much larger quantities.
- The third brother (Dishonorable Dan) adopted the city dwellers' unhealthy diet.
- The fourth brother (Addicted Albert) ate all foods in excess.

Over time, Addicted Albert became ill while Excessive Eddie and Dishonorable Dan saw their health diminished. But Moderate Mike remained fit and vigorous.

The Parable of the Four Brothers Explained

As you probably guessed, food represents screen time in this parable.

Life on the farm represents the world as it has always been. Screens did not exist. The move to the city represents our new life with screens.

Now on to the brothers:

Brother #1 (Moderate Mike) represents the person who uses screens wisely, in moderation, with noble intent—leaving plenty of time for real life.

Brother #2 (Excessive Eddie) represents the person who *overuses* screens. He's deploying them for innocent purposes, but his screen use is displacing important things and diminishing his quality of life.

Brother #3 (Dishonorable Dan) represents the person who *misuses* screens for unhealthy purposes. He is watching and doing things online that corrode his character.

Brother #4 (Addicted Albert) represents the person whose screen life is so out of control that it's destroying his real life, and his addiction is negatively affecting those around him.

Let's look at the brothers in graphic form:

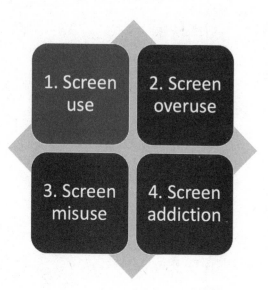

So which brother are you? Be honest. Which box do you find yourself in? Are you in control of your screen life, or do your screens control you?

Before you read any further, I'm going to ask you to go to my website and take the Four Brothers online quiz (www.DavidMurrow. com/screens/tools). It only takes a few minutes. I promise to keep your identity and your quiz results confidential.

Why didn't I just print the quiz in the book, you ask? Technology is changing so rapidly that a printed quiz would soon be out of date. Hosting the quiz online allows me to update it as screen life evolves. In the following chapters, I'll be directing you to my website for the same reason. I keep updated lists of the latest digital tools that can help you master real life. If you'd like to explore the site, visit www. DavidMurrow.com/screens.

3.2

Be Like Mike: How to Stay Afloat

A l Menconi has been speaking to groups of students and young adults for more than thirty years about the ways their entertainment choices affect their lives. Invariably, someone comes up to him after he speaks and says these words: *But it doesn't affect me!*

Robert spends forty-plus hours a week gaming. But it doesn't affect him.

Lydia checks her phone more than 150 times a day. But it doesn't affect her.

Grayson views violent porn every night. But it doesn't affect him.

Adriana watches TV nine hours a day. But it doesn't affect her.

Humans are masters of denial. What we feed our minds affects us just as much or more than what we feed our bodies.

The first step in Moderate Mike's pathway to freedom was simple honesty: It *does* affect me. Mike recognized and admitted his screen life was negatively impacting his real life. Then he took the second step: he decided to do something about it.

The next three chapters are full of "somethings" you can do to help you stay afloat when everyone around you is drowning in screen time. They are loosely organized by brother. This chapter contains positive steps *any* screen user would benefit from taking.

Focus on Eliminating Mindless Screen Time

Honestly, this might be all you have to do to restore balance in your life. Simply focus on cutting out mindless activities such as web surfing, watching TV, or scrolling through social media. Target the low-value screen activities you thoughtlessly turn to and you'll recover a ton of valuable time and energy.

The next time you have a couple of minutes to kill, don't reach for your phone. Instead ask yourself, "What's something fun or profitable I could be doing for the next two minutes?" Grab a coffee. Practice noticing things: the color of a flower, cloud formations, or various styles of architecture. Stretch your muscles. Daydream. Pray for a friend or relative. Close your eyes and rest your brain. Look for someone to smile at or be kind to. Every little moment you spend in the real world keeps you in sight of the shore.

Change Your Self-Talk

Let's say you're a chocolate lover. Every day after work, you dive into a box of truffles, pralines, or bonbons. Predictably, your weight goes up, and you begin developing diabetes. Your physician gives you a stern warning: you need to give up chocolate.

You come home from the doctor's office, look at that box of chocolates on the counter, and the voice in your head says, "I can't eat chocolate because the doctor said no." You're defeated already, because you've characterized your newfound discipline as something that's being imposed on you by somebody else.

So instead of telling yourself, "I can't eat chocolate," say, "I don't eat chocolate." The decision to abstain is not something you're being forced to do; it's a decision you've made. Being controlled is debilitating, but setting your own boundaries is empowering.

Here are some examples of positive screen self-talk:

- I choose to turn on the TV only when I'm watching a specific show. Then I shut it off.
- I like the health benefits of spending time outdoors instead of playing video games.
- I turn my phone off at night. A good night's sleep makes me sharper.
- I avoid sexually stimulating content because it leads to real-life loneliness.
- I check my email just once a day.

Set a Timer

This one's a no-brainer. Use your smartphone's voice-activated timer to place a limit on your screen time. For example, the next time you decide to play video games or surf the web, pull out your phone and say, "Hey Siri, (or Google), set a timer for forty-five minutes." When the bell sounds, get back to real life.

How to Control the Urge to Check Your Device

When are you most tempted to check your phone? When you're engaged in a dull, routine, or undesirable task. Last week I had to pull some tax documents together. Sorting through papers and entering numbers in a spreadsheet is not my idea of entertainment. My web browser practically sang to me: *"Click over here, David. I have dopamine for you!"*

The next time you need to concentrate on a less-than-thrilling task, put your devices in Do Not Disturb mode and stream some motivating music into the room. You'll complete the task much more quickly and earn a well-deserved splash of dopamine when it's all done.

If you're the type to absentmindedly reach for your phone, try placing a rubber band on your wrist. Each time your hand glides toward your phone, snap yourself. *Ouch!*

Reward Yourself for Abstaining

If you're into pleasure rather than pain, try a reward system. For example, if you go an entire evening without any screen time, do something nice for yourself. Put a few dollars into your coffee fund. Treat yourself to an ice cream (on your way back from the gym, of course). Couples who abstain from screens together can reward each other in so many wonderful ways. Celebrate your small triumphs.

Screen Sabbath

Many religions call their adherents to observe a weekly sabbath, a day of rest in which normal work and routines are put aside. Some people are extending this ancient regimen to their screens.

I've recently begun observing a "soft screen sabbath" every Sunday. I call it *soft* because I'm not legalistic about it. For example, I still carry my phone and use it to make calls, send texts, or navigate when I get lost. But I don't use it for any other purpose. My normally busy laptop gets the day off. And I avoid TV—except to watch an occasional game during football season. (I was born in Green Bay, so if the Packers are on TV, I usually watch.)

With my screen life minimized, I focus on developing my real life every Sunday. I try to interact with as many flesh-and-blood people as I can. My wife and I attend church, catch up with friends, and grab something to eat on the way home. I recently re-subscribed to the local newspaper, which I read cover to cover. I also try to get in some recreation—like taking a walk or bike ride, going to the pool, or doing something with my hands. I make old-fashioned phone calls to people I care about. And there's usually time to sneak in a nap. By Sunday night, I feel more connected to my wife, my friends, and the real world. I open my laptop Monday morning refreshed and ready to write again.

What Not to Do: Become a Digital Hermit

As evidence of technology's negative effects continues to mount, some people are fighting back to the extreme. Wary of overstimulating their brains, some tech-savvy young adults are getting into "dopamine fasting."[1] This ill-advised fad has influenced people to avoid not only screen time, but anything that might give them an ounce of pleasure— such as rich foods, friendly conversation, or even making eye contact with a stranger. The idea is to "heal" their brains by denying themselves any experience that might stimulate their gray matter.

The problem isn't dopamine—it's an unnatural excess of dopamine from an artificially overstimulated brain. The constant scene changes of TV, the flitting from one web page to another, or scrolling through endless posts—these are the wolves that are revving up our brains.

The way to heal your brain is to do the things humans have done for thousands of years: Get out and experience the real world. Be among people. Let your mind wander. Smile at someone. Talk to a friend or make a new one. Prepare a good meal and enjoy every bite. Give thanks for our wonderful, technologically advanced world.

3.3

How Excessive Eddie Cut Back

When you've read as many books about screens as I have, you begin to notice a familiar pattern. Authors often tell tales of extreme addiction, like the Taiwanese man who died of a heart attack after playing *League of Legends* for twenty-three hours straight, the American teenager who took her own life after binge-watching a TV show about suicide, the Brazilian man who walked into the path of an oncoming bus while playing a game on his phone, or the Chinese youths who wear diapers so they don't have to interrupt their gaming sessions.

We read these stories, and we let ourselves off the hook. *I'm not wearing diapers, so I guess I'm OK,* we say to ourselves.

You may not be an out-of-control screen addict, but I hope by now you recognize that you're using screens more than you'd like. Excessive Eddie's problem was portion control. He ate beneficial foods—but in enormous quantities. In a similar vein, many of us use our devices with noble intent, but we're using them too much, and that's keeping us from fully engaging in real life. Here are some tips that will help you slim down your screen time.

Tame Your TV Habit
Keep the TV Off and Say NO to Channel Surfing

People tend to turn on the TV and leave it on in the background, not realizing what a mental distraction it is. Eventually, they sit down and channel surf until they find something to watch. Then they watch the next show and the next. Before they know it, they've lost their entire evening to the tube. Plus, they've been exposed to dozens of commercials for things they don't need.

The best way to cut back on TV is to keep it turned off until you're ready to watch a specific program. When the show is over, have the discipline to turn it off. It's easy once you get into the habit. Just keep the remote handy and apply gentle pressure to the red button.

Replace TV Noise with Real Talk and Music

My wife admits to using TV and radio noise to feel less isolated when she's home alone. I recently challenged her to trade artificial companionship for the real thing. Now when she feels alone, she calls a friend instead of firing up the flat screen. I've also gotten her hooked on playing relaxing background music that soothes her brain instead of TV noise that keeps her on alert.

Place the TV in a Separate Room

When our kids were little, we wanted to teach them that television was not our family's go-to activity. So we put the TV in the basement. Our family room was reserved for sitting and visiting, reading books, kids' play, and lots of roughhousing. I'm happy to report none of my kids grew up to be heavy TV watchers. If you have the space, make your common living space a television-free zone. I have friends who keep their TV in a closet when they're not watching it. Modern flat screens are lightweight and fairly easy to store. Just be careful not to squeeze the edges or you can break the screen.

Drop Your Cable/Satellite Subscription

Cable and satellite TV subscribers often feel trapped. They're paying a huge monthly bill for their services, so they feel they have to watch a lot of TV to get their money's worth. Or they are forced to purchase an expensive cable package to get one or two channels they feel they can't live without.

Folks, we live in the cord-cutting era. Subscribe to three or four streaming services. You end up paying about the same or less than you would for a cable subscription, but now you can watch your favorite programs on demand, commercial-free. And you'll never miss an episode because of a power outage or an improperly programmed DVR.

If you're planning to cut the cord, try connecting an antenna to your TV. I did that last year and was surprised at how many over-the-air channels are now available. These free channels can help as you wean yourself off cable.

Beat the Cliffhanger Trap

Many TV shows end each episode with a "cliffhanger"—an unresolved plot twist that makes you want to keep watching. The most famous TV cliffhanger of all time was broadcast on March 21, 1980, when the villainous J. R. Ewing was gunned down by an unknown assailant during the final episode of season three of the CBS series *Dallas*. All of America asked, "Who shot J. R.?" The largest audience in television history (up to that point) tuned in on November 21, 1980, to find out whodunnit.

TV shows still have cliffhangers, but we no longer have to wait eight months for the next episode. With streaming entertainment, it's more like eight seconds. The next installment plays automatically—and that can be a problem.

Cliffhangers lead to binge watching. The suspense is killing us, so we start viewing the next episode, which ends with another cliffhanger, so we watch another episode, and so on. Before we know it, we've been sitting alone in the dark for five hours. It's 2:30 in the morning, and we've got to be at work by 7:00 a.m.

Professor Adam Alter has devised a simple way to beat cliffhangers.[1] When you come to one, go ahead and watch the first few minutes of the next episode until the cliffhanger is resolved. Then pause the video and call it a night. Do the same for the next episode. My wife and I employ this strategy when we just can't stand the suspense. It works as long we have the discipline to stop the video as soon as the mystery is revealed.

How to Keep Your TV from Interrupting Sleep

Do you have a television in the bedroom? According to a National Sleep Foundation poll, 60 percent of Americans watch TV right before nodding off. A survey by LG Electronics claims that nearly two-thirds of Americans regularly fall asleep with the TV on.[2] My late father-in-law was one of these people. He'd switch on the set, and fifteen minutes later he'd be snoring away.

But he also slept fitfully. I suspect that the same TV that lulled him to sleep also kept his nervous system on alert. We're meant to sleep in darkness and silence, not with the sound of commercials bombarding our ears.

Doctors recommend we not interact with screens in the hour before we go to bed. Our brains need a chance to relax before we fall asleep.

Here are some tips for better sleep:

1. If you don't already have a TV in your bedroom, don't get one. You don't want the bluish light of a television

set in your bedroom. It's better to watch TV in the living room and then retire to the bedroom.

2. Avoid all interactive media in the hour before you sleep, especially lean-forward activities such as video gaming or posting to social media.

3. If you must watch something before going to sleep, use a laptop or tablet that's capable of changing color temperature. For example, all Apple devices have a feature called Night Shift that filters out the blue light our eyes and brains associate with daytime. I have Night Shift programmed to come on every evening at 8 p.m. All my screens suddenly "shift" from a bluish hue to an orange one. I've noticed that both my wife and I fall asleep more quickly and easily since we've begun Night Shifting our devices close to bedtime.

Take Control of Your Phone
Use a Screen Time Tracking App

Most of us have no idea how much time we spend on our devices. Fortunately, there are more than a dozen free and paid apps that track your screen time across all your devices. AntiSocial is one of the most popular apps for Android. It compares your screen time to the screen time of other people your age and gender, so you'll know how you stack up. It can keep track of your unlocks, phone time, phone usage, and screen time by app, and it delivers a weekly report right to your device or to the device of an accountability partner.

One of the cleverest anti-phone checking apps is called Forest. It trains you not to look at your device by turning your screen into a virtual tree planting nursery. You plant a seed and set a gestation period, say two hours. During that time, a tree will grow on your screen. If you use your phone any time during those 120 minutes, the tree will wither and die. The more times you abstain, the bigger your forest grows. "I used to check my phone fifty or sixty times a day," said twenty-two-year-old Adriana. "But when I pick up my phone and see that tree growing, I think to myself, 'I can't kill that poor little tree.'"

Family and friends can plant trees together to keep each other accountable (couples on dates should always use this feature to avoid phubbing). Forest even allows you to earn virtual coins that can be cashed in to support the planting of real trees in Sub-Saharan Africa.

I keep a list of time trackers at my website: www.DavidMurrow. com/screens/tools.

Stop the Buzz: How to Keep Your Phone from Distracting You

The less often your phone chirps or buzzes, the less likely you are to look at it. Here's the easy way to tame your alerts:

- Go into your device's settings>notifications menu and turn them all off.
- Go through the list of apps and turn notifications back on for the alerts you actually want.
- Make the notifications as unobtrusive as possible by turning off sounds and vibrations. Also, keep them off your lock screen.

Which notifications should be on? Calendars is a definite ON. You don't want to miss appointments. Most people leave chat and SMS (text) notifications ON. I like getting notifications when I travel, so I leave notifications ON for my travel apps (airlines, for example).

What about notifications at night? Even if they don't wake you up, all that buzzing, glimmering, and chirping can stimulate your brain just enough to interrupt your sleep cycle. Simply turn your phone off, place it in airplane mode, or charge it in another room while you slumber.

If you insist on sleeping next to your phone, both Apple and Android phones offer a customizable Do Not Disturb mode that can virtually silence your device, allowing only the most important calls and texts to come through. For example, my Do Not Disturb starts every evening at 9:00 p.m. and concludes at 7:00 a.m. Between those hours, my phone turns into a brick—almost.

Here's why Do Not Disturb is better for me than airplane mode or powering off: important calls can still get through. Do Not Disturb can be programmed to allow calls and messages from people on your "favorites" list any time of day or night. For example, my daughter was out late the other night and had car trouble at 11:00 p.m. Because she is on my favorites list, the call came through. Had I turned my phone off or put it in airplane mode, she would not have been able to reach me. Do Not Disturb can also be set to ring through if someone calls three times in rapid succession.

I've recently started using Do Not Disturb on my iPhone and Mac while I am working. My friend Chip goes even further, putting his phone in airplane mode while he's in the office and reconnecting during his lunch break. "If people really want to get ahold of me, they'll dial my desk landline number," he says.

Leave Your Device to Its Own Devices

Rather than carrying their devices at all times, some people place them on a charging station while they're not using them. My friend Brie has a wireless charger in her living room. As soon as she gets home, she puts her Android handset on the stand and leaves it there until she leaves the house the next morning. This approach has several advantages: the device stays charged, it never disturbs her sleep, and she always knows where it is. "I'm kinda old school," she said. "I grew up answering a phone on the wall, and I like having it in a certain place." Brie has discovered she is much less likely to pull the phone out of her pocket if it's not in her pocket in the first place.

Sleep experts advise us not to bring our phones into the bedroom with us. Since my phone automatically goes into Do Not Disturb mode at 9:00 p.m., this isn't really a problem for me. I'm not the type to check my phone during the night, and I like having the phone near in case of an emergency. However, if the urge to check your phone in bed is overwhelming, set up a charging station in another room.

Never Touch Your Phone in the Bathroom

Toilet time is perfect for giving your brain a rest. Your body is immobile—your mind should be too. Just let your attention wander or take a moment to reflect and be thankful for all the blessings you've been given. Don't know where to start? How about the wonders of modern plumbing, or two-ply toilet paper? You can take it from there...

There are practical reasons not to pull your phone out in the loo. What if you drop it in the bowl or onto a hard tile floor? Not to mention the hygienic concerns that arise from touching a device after using the toilet. Abigail Abrams writes in *Time* magazine:

> One of the worst places to use your phone is in the bathroom. When toilets flush, they spread germs everywhere, which is how phones end up with fecal bacteria like E. coli. "Taking a cell phone into the bathroom and then leaving with it is kind of like going in, not washing your hands and then coming back out," [University of Michigan associate professor Emily] Martin says. "It's the same level of concern."[3]

Even if you wash your hands, you can still transfer germs to and from your phone. Researchers at the University of Arizona found that cell phones carry ten times more bacteria than the typical toilet seat.[4]

Make Your Phone Black-and-White

Want to make your phone less enticing? Eliminate the color. Instagram photos aren't nearly as interesting in grayscale. iPhones can toggle quickly between color and grayscale by triple-clicking the home button.

Use Real Clocks to Tell Time

In ancient times (before mobile phones), people used to wear watches on their wrists to tell the time. These can still be purchased at the local discount stores for fewer than fifteen dollars. Believe it or not, glancing at your wrist is faster and easier than pulling out your phone. And while you're at the store, pick up an old-school alarm clock for the bedside. I have one that projects the time onto the ceiling. Try doing *that* with a smartphone!

Delete Social Media Apps from Your Phone

This isn't as radical as it sounds. You don't really need social media in your pocket. You can maintain an active social media presence from your tablet or laptop alone.

Try this strategy: delete the parent social apps (Facebook, Instagram, etc.) but keep their associated messenger apps (like Facebook Messenger). That way your social media BFFs can still reach out via direct message, but the temptation to mindlessly scroll your feed will be gone.

Productivity Tips
If You Work from Home, Set Office Hours

My office is in my home. It's a five-second commute from my bedroom to my desk. If the traffic is heavy (such as a laundry basket in the doorway), it takes me eight seconds. Since my office is so accessible and I tend to be a night owl, I'm constantly tempted to work into the evening. But I'm learning that I'm more productive if I set a stop time each day. Tonight, that time is 6:00 p.m. I'll grab something to eat, go down to the gym, and have a relaxing swim before bed tonight. Since my wife is out of town, I'll check my phone briefly to see if she wants to chat, do some reading (from a paper book), and then it's off to the Land of Nod.

Log Out of Social Media While You Work

I manage several very active Facebook pages, so I'm constantly tempted to check how my posts are doing. Then I see an interesting post. And another. Before I know it, I've wasted thirty minutes or more mindlessly searching for novelty. So I've set a limit: I allow myself to check social media before I start writing, at my lunch break, and when I'm finished in the evening.

How do I keep my readers engaged through the day? I use Facebook's Creator Studio in the morning to schedule posts to show up at regular intervals—even in the middle of the night for my readers in Australia and Europe. That way I'm able to feed the social media monster around the clock without sacrificing much work time.

Tame Your Email with a Two-Inbox Strategy

I had no idea what I was signing up for on June 12, 1998. That's the day I got my first email account, a free address on Yahoo! I shared my address with a few tech-savvy friends and signed up for a couple of newsletters. By the end of June, I was getting three to four emails a day.

Five years later, I had more than 50,000 unread emails in my Yahoo! inbox. Every morning, I woke up to about 150 new messages. I was beginning to miss important personal and business emails because my inbox was so stuffed with newsletters, advertisements, and fundraising appeals.

Here's how I tamed my email tiger in about an hour without unsubscribing to anything: I already had a free email account from

Apple that I didn't use much (every iPhone comes with a free iCloud account). This became my new *primary* address. I give my primary address out to my priority contacts such as family, friends, business associates, doctors, financial institutions, etc. I check my primary email several times a day. Meanwhile, I still use my old, reliable Yahoo! address when I sign up for new accounts, newsletters, etc. I visit that inbox once a day.

I've posted a detailed plan titled "How to tame your email with a second inbox" complete with diagrams at my website: www. DavidMurrow.com/screens/tools.

One more thing: I've turned off all email notifications on my laptop, tablet, and phone. Email is almost never urgent, so there's no reason to be pinged the moment a message comes in.

Use Screen Maps to Preview Your Route and Then Navigate the Old-Fashioned Way

Our phones are great navigators, and as a result, we're losing the ability to find our way around. Each time we blindly follow our devices to a destination, we miss an opportunity to fortify our brains. M. R. O'Connor writes in the *Washington Post*:

> In a study published in *Nature Communications* in 2017, researchers asked subjects to navigate a virtual simulation of London's Soho neighborhood and monitored their brain activity, specifically the hippocampus, which is integral to spatial navigation. Those who were guided by directions showed less activity in this part of the brain than participants who navigated without the device. "The hippocampus makes an internal map of the environment and this map becomes active only when you are engaged in navigating and not using GPS," Amir-Homayoun Javadi, one of the study's authors, told me.

Studies have long shown the hippocampus is highly susceptible to experience. (London's taxi drivers famously have greater gray-matter volume in the hippocampus as a consequence of memorizing the city's labyrinthine streets.) Meanwhile, atrophy in that part of the brain is linked to devastating conditions, including post-traumatic stress disorder and Alzheimer's disease.[5]

Advice: Next time you need to go somewhere, use GPS to plan the best route. Study the overview. Note the names of streets and highways. Picture your turns and straightaways. Then mute the voice and try to get there on your own. If you get lost, turn the voice prompts back on again.

■   ■   ■

New screen temptations emerge all the time, so Excessive Eddies must stay constantly vigilant. I track these wolves at my website, along with successful strategies to keep them in check. Stop by for a (brief) visit: www.DavidMurrow.com/screens. Then get back to real life.

3.4

Dishonorable Dan and the Poisons of the Screen World

The haggard old woman held out a shiny red apple. "It's a magic wishing apple," she said. "One bite, and all your dreams come true!" The fruit looked delicious, and Snow White didn't want to be disagreeable. She took a bite and immediately fell under the spell of the Evil Queen.

This classic fairy tale captures the sad reality of Brother #3, Dishonorable Dan. When he left the farm and moved to the city, Dan found exotic new foods that looked and tasted delicious. The more he ate, the more accustomed his brain became to the satisfying emotions these foods generated. The rush of pleasure tricked Dan's mind into believing he was doing something good for his health, when in reality he was slowly poisoning himself.

The screen world is full of poisoned apples—enticing content that promises to make our dreams come true. But the moment we bite, we fall under the poisoned apples' spell. The more we consume these apples, the more they toxify our character, our relationships, and our ability to function in real life.

In this chapter, I'm going to reveal seven of the screen world's most tempting poisoned apples. And in the next chapter, we'll discuss some ways to avoid taking that first bite.

Poisoned Apple #1: The Deep Web and the Dark Web

There's a companion network to the World Wide Web known as the deep web. Deep websites don't show up on search engines. Kaspersky Lab estimates about 90 percent of all websites are hosted on the deep web, and most of them are perfectly legitimate. Companies, non-profit organizations, and academic institutions use the deep web for their internal networks (intranets). This keeps prying eyes out of private data and facilitates confidential communication and collaboration. The deep web is also a testing ground for pre-release software, while journalists and dissidents use it to preserve anonymity.

But within the deep web there's another subset of sites known as the dark web—a cesspool of unlawful activity. Dark websites are also hidden from search engines and cannot be accessed from a typical browser such as Chrome, Safari, or Firefox. You can buy almost anything on the dark web, including illegal drugs, guns, hacked passwords, fake IDs, and stolen credit card information. Want to hire a hitman, launder money, or engage in sex trafficking? It's all available on the dark web.

But the dark web's biggest draw is its vast library of child pornography. About 80 percent of the traffic on the dark web is related to pedophilia, according to a 2014 study from the University of Portsmouth.[1] That figure is a very rough estimate, as these secretive sites are notoriously hard to track. But if it is anywhere near correct, the dark web functions primarily as a vast marketplace dealing in images of abused and tormented children.

The dark web is not a place to poke around out of curiosity. Any information you share could be used to blackmail you. You could end up with a nasty computer virus, or your personal data could be stolen. You might accidentally stumble across illegal content that could make you an accessory to a crime. And you are very likely to encounter content you can never "unsee." According to Kaspersky Labs:

> [T]here's virtually no law enforcement presence down in the Dark. This means anything—even material well outside the bounds of good taste and common decency—can be found online. This includes offensive, illegal "adult" content that would likely scar the viewer for life.[2]

Solution: If you are visiting the dark web, stop. There's nothing down there you need. You're putting yourself at great risk.

Poisoned Apple #2: Cyberbullying

In the real world, bullies can only torment those in close physical proximity. But the screen world allows bullies to harm their victims via text, email, or social media. While a cyberbully can't physically injure a victim via screen, he or she can inflict emotional damage or encourage their targets to hurt themselves. That's what happened to fifteen-year-old Jack Padilla, a high school freshman from suburban Denver. Padilla was ruthlessly bullied in person and via direct message. His tormentors threatened to shoot Padilla if he didn't kill himself, which he eventually did in 2019.[3]

Cyberbullies can now broadcast their bile to a worldwide audience, posting falsehoods about their victims for all to see. Instead of blunt fists or sharp tongues, today's bullies use camera phones to capture embarrassing photos and videos and post them to social media. Fifteen-year-old Tovonna Holton-Teamer of Florida shot herself to death after a classmate filmed her taking a shower and posted the video on Snapchat.[4]

You've never done something so horrible, have you? Let's hope not. But you may still have participated in cyberbullying without realizing it. Have you ever:

- Posted false or misleading information about someone in an attempt to embarrass them or exact revenge?
- Threatened or harassed someone via text, instant message, or social media?
- Revealed private information about another person online (doxing)?
- Falsely accused someone of online harassment (playing the victim) to get them kicked off social media?
- Participated in an online hot-or-not poll to gauge whether someone is attractive or ugly?
- Text-attacked someone (filling their inbox with harassing or gibberish texts)?
- Impersonated someone else online and posted shameful content in their name?
- Sent malicious code or spyware to a victim?
- Posted or forwarded an embarrassing photo of someone?

If you've done any of these things, go back in time and relive your emotions the moment you pressed "send" or "enter." You probably experienced a mixture of white-hot pleasure along with a twinge of guilt. That twinge was your conscience. Listen to it, if not for the sake of common decency, then for your own self-preservation. Remember, everything you post on a screen may be permanently archived. Even the disappearing stuff can be captured via screenshot. You may think the web gives you anonymity, but sometimes it does not. A single mean-spirited tweet could cost you a relationship, a scholarship, or a career—years or even decades later.

Solution: Apologize to those you've bullied. Where appropriate, make amends.

Poisoned Apple #3: Spreading Falsehoods Online

Just this morning as I was mindlessly scrolling through Facebook (yes, I still do that on occasion, but only for a few minutes), I came across a meme showing former president Barack Obama awarding the Presidential Medal of Freedom to disgraced movie mogul Harvey Weinstein.

I could tell the photo was a poorly executed Photoshop hack job. I checked the list of medal recipients on Wikipedia. Weinstein's name did not appear. So I replied to the friend who posted the false meme, asking him to delete it. He refused, saying, "It may not be factually correct, but this is the kind of stuff Obama did to our country for eight years."

I also have a friend who's very sour on church. Anytime some wacko preacher with a congregation of twenty people says or does something unloving or unhinged, she's sure to post it on her social feed. Her likeminded friends leave outraged comments, confirming their mutual suspicion that every Christian is a crazy, narrow-minded bigot.

To my partisan friends, social media is more about affirmation than information. They search for posts that confirm their opinions and then repost them to their feeds. Friends gather to "like" these posts, forming a chorus of indignation and self-righteousness. Whether these posts are true or not is beside the point.

A report from BBC and CBS confirms both liberals and conservatives are prone to post fake news that confirms their preexisting biases:[5]

"It [fake news] affects both the right and the left. It affects educated and uneducated. So the stereotypes of it being simply right-wing and simply uneducated are 100 percent not true," says Jeff Green, who is the CEO of Trade Desk, an internet advertising company that was recently commissioned by American TV channel CBS to investigate who is reading and sharing fake news online.

"On the left if you're consuming fake news you're 34 times more likely than the general population to be a college graduate," says Green.

If you're on the right, he says, you're 18 times more likely than the general population to be in the top 20 percent of income earners.

And the study revealed another disturbing trend: the more you consume fake news, the more likely you are to vote. It's "fascinating and frightening at the same time," says Green.

If you spread falsehoods online, you are a liar. And you may actually be reposting material placed by foreign trolls who are trying to inflame, confuse, and undermine democratic societies.

So before you post, check the source. Don't repost articles from unknown or highly partisan websites. And before you post or retweet, check the dateline of the story. In the wake of basketball star Kobe Bryant's death in a helicopter crash, another story began circulating on social media: deadly helicopter crash kills thirty U.S. Marines in Iraq. The story was true, but the crash had taken place in 2005. People had heard about Bryant and went to the internet, searching for "helicopter crash." Google served up this fifteen-year-old story, and folks began posting it as if it were breaking news.

Solution: Check the accuracy and timeliness of everything you post before you post it.

Poisoned Apple #4: Disrobing in Front of a Camera

So you're thinking of taking pictures of yourself unclothed and texting them to your lover. It's called *sexting,* and there are so many ways it can go wrong. Here are five:

- Phones get hacked
- Images get shared
- Kids get into their parents' phones (Oops!)
- Camera rolls automatically upload to other devices (Oops again!)
- If you break up, your ex has a catalog of images of your naked body

Couples that sext also experience a higher degree of conflict, lower levels of commitment, feel less secure, and are more likely to engage in infidelity.[6] Sexting has cost at least two members of the U.S. Congress their jobs: New York representative Anthony Weiner stepped down after he was discovered sending nude photos to a teen girl, while California representative Katie Hill resigned after her estranged husband published selfies of her engaging in sexual acts with staffers.

When adults sext, it's foolish, but when kids sext, it's tragic. More than 15 percent of eight-year-old girls have been exposed to sexting.[7] By the time they are thirteen years old, 40 percent of children have either sent or received such an image. Kids being kids, they show these nude images to their friends. Soon every boy in class has seen Tammy topless. When Tammy finds out, she's upset, depressed, and quite possibly suicidal.

Three words: sexting is stupid. Here are three more: don't do it.

A close cousin of sexting is sextortion. Here's how that works: A guy begins chatting with an attractive woman online. But the woman is actually a cybercriminal. The criminal begins talking sexy with the man and convinces him to disrobe and masturbate in front of his webcam. The criminal then plays back the video for the horrified victim and threatens to post it online if he doesn't send money.

Solution: Never undress in front of a camera or webcam.

Poisoned Apple #5: Trolling and Online Attacks

It happens all the time: somebody posts something on social media that's so outrageous you feel you have to respond.

You don't.

It's not your job to change people's minds or correct their misconceptions. There's no point in arguing with an ideologue. If you engage with an argumentative person on social media, the algorithms are just going to serve you more of their posts.

Social media feuds are often just virtue signaling. We're not trying to change minds; instead, we're demonstrating our superior intellect to fellow members of our tribe. We feel smug together as we look down on those unenlightened dolts who are too stupid to see things as clearly as we do.

Resist the urge to get into online shouting matches. Avoid the comments sections that follow articles—that's where the trolls hang out. Don't become a member of the "pajamahadeen" sitting in your nightwear, banging out opinions on your keyboard.

Some people derive sick pleasure from trolling. They intentionally start quarrels or provoke people by posting inflammatory or off-topic material. The troll's goal is to sow discord and get people fighting with one another. Leave the trolls alone. Don't give them the satisfaction of getting your goat.

The book of Proverbs says, "A soft answer turns away wrath, but a harsh word stirs up anger." There are plenty of people stirring up anger online. Be the person who turns away wrath. If you respond, do so calmly and graciously. Don't attack the messenger, impugn their character, or question their intelligence.

Solution: Resist the urge to participate in online knife fights.

Poisoned Apple #6: Crude, Cruel, and Degrading Stuff

When you enter flawed data into a computer program, flawed data come out of the machine. That's where we get the saying "Garbage in, garbage out."

So it is with screen content. Studies have demonstrated a link between the consumption of crude, cruel, and degrading screen content and increased promiscuity, violence, and substance abuse among children and adolescents.[8] If tens of millions of us are regularly loading our brains with garbage, why are we surprised by the decline of civility and kindness?

Speaking of garbage, the father of trashy television is a man by the name of Jerry Springer. His tabloid TV show was a cross between Dr. Phil and World Wrestling Entertainment. Springer welcomed guests on his set to talk about their relationship problems. Before long they were brawling, clawing, hair-pulling, and cursing each other while a studio audience taunted, booed, and cheered, chanting "JER-RY, JER-RY!" The fights were obviously staged, yet morbidly fascinating. In 1998, *The Jerry Springer Show* was America's top-rated daytime talk show.[9]

But this televised freak show was finally canceled after twenty-seven seasons. It was no match for the internet's around-the-clock displays of human depravity. Stuart Heritage writes in *The Guardian*:[10]

> The show's sense of mob rule, where audiences are whipped up into a terrifying froth and urged to come down as hard as possible on subjects they know little about, has been

replicated on Twitter. Springer's "final thought," which attempted to paper over the atrocities of a given episode with trite platitudes, is present in every motivational quote posted to Instagram. And what is Springer's furious ratings-at-any-cost attitude if not a clear precursor to clickbait?

Since the early days of radio and television, the Federal Communications Commission has policed the airwaves to keep obscene, indecent, and profane broadcasts off the air. But cable television and streaming services operate under no such restrictions. Home Box Office (HBO) is famous for lacing shows with nudity, violence, foul language, and cruelty that do little to advance the plot. HBO normalized on-screen nudity through a cinematic technique known as *sexposition:* placing naked bodies in the background of a shot while the main characters ignore them.

The more we are exposed to violence, cruelty, and sexual exploitation, the more our brains come to accept these things as normal. Their power to arouse or outrage us weakens. The horrific becomes the expected—trees instead of wolves.

Do you doubt this? Then how do you explain the popularity of animal crush videos, in which small mammals such as rabbits or cats are mercilessly executed on camera?[11] These videos are illegal, but they thrive on the dark web. I cannot imagine why anyone would want to witness such wanton cruelty—unless their consciences were already dulled by having viewed other forms of on-screen brutality.

If you come across crude, cruel, indecent, or degrading screen content, you're likely to experience a strange mix of revulsion and curiosity. Remember, your brain is wired for novelty, and sicko content is certainly novel. Don't take that intrigue as a green light to go further. Stop while you still recognize the wolf for what it is—a threat to your mental health.

Solution: Talk to a trusted confidant, counselor, or pastor about your viewing habits. Details to come in the next chapter.

Poisoned Apple #7: Pornography

As I wrote in Chapter 2.11, porn used to be hard to find. Today eleven-year-olds carry vast libraries of it in their pockets. Three of the web's top ten most visited addresses are porn sites.[12]

Chances are you didn't seek out porn. It found you. Many people have their first exposure to porn as children when it pops onto their screens uninvited. It's not a fair fight. Porn quickly overwhelms the novelty centers of a youngster's still-developing brain. Repeated exposure carves deep neural pathways that make porn extremely addictive.

Solution: It's in our next chapter.

3.5

How Albert, Dan, and Eddie Can Find Freedom

So you've tried all the practical steps I've been sharing in the past few chapters, and nothing's changing. You're still picking up your phone sixty times a day. Social media dominates your thoughts. You can't seem to control your video gaming, no matter what you try. You feel powerless to stop the flood of erotic, porn-fueled images that commandeer your thoughts.

This would seem to indicate you're an Addicted Albert. That doesn't make you a failure. Or weak. Or pitiful. Everything about screens and their content is made to be addictive—programmed to keep you clicking, swiping, reading, scrolling, shooting, posting, and watching. Like Max from our first parable, you simply swam too far from the shore, failed to recognize the threat posed by the jellyfish, and were carried out to sea by tides you didn't know were there.

Those tides are only going to get stronger. During the global shutdowns of 2020, we learned how easy, convenient, and earth-friendly it was to live on our screens. Employees ditched their morning commutes and worked from home. CEOs realized their workers could be just as productive collaborating on screen. Pollution levels plummeted. Every college student on earth discovered the convenience of attending classes online. And for the first time, millions of churchgoers worshipped from the comfort of their living rooms.

Having recognized all these benefits, how can we possibly go back? Investors will pour billions into inventions that keep us isolated from one another. Entrepreneurs and innovators will devise new ways to experience life via screen. In such a world, screen overuse, misuse, and addiction will only increase. It will take a great deal of intentionality and support to swim against this tide. But you can do it. Think of this chapter as a rescue plan to help you make it back to shore.

Self-Directed Digital Detox

In the case of heavy screen users such as Addicted Albert, cutting back a bit just won't cut it.

Albert's brain has become dependent on the constant trickle of dopamine his screens provide. The only way he can retrain his brain to seek normal levels of stimulation is to go cold turkey by eliminating *all* screen use from his life for a predetermined length of time. This is referred to as a *digital detox*. A detox retrains the brain to expect a normal level of novelty and stimulation, so Albert can take pleasure in real-world sights, sounds, and experiences again.

How long should a detox take? The longer the better. You're trying to reverse the effects of years of overstimulation. A weekend is the bare minimum. Seven days is better. An entire month is ideal. The longer your brain has to habituate itself to screen-free living, the stronger your resolve will be. Even a brief detox can lead to big changes. Many people begin to reacclimate to real life within hours.

Even if your addiction is rooted in a single device or activity, I strongly recommend you remove ALL screen use from your life during the detox period. Addicts often cut out one screen addiction (video games, for example) but then immerse themselves in another (binge-watching TV or pornography). Instead of healing their brains, addicts just substitute one source of stimulation for another.

The easiest way to break up with your screens is to get out of town. Leave all your technology behind. All of it. Even your phone. If you must stay in touch during your detox, purchase or rent a pushbutton prepaid phone with a zero data plan and forward your calls to it. Buy a paper map and hit the road.

Obviously, the best places to detox are sleepy locales with poor internet service. Ideally, you want to get away to someplace natural. Backcountry tent camping is a particularly good way to detox because it requires so many survival activities. That keeps your hands busy and your mind off your screens.

If you want to get outdoors but don't want to rough it too much, you could rent a cabin without TV. Church camps are another great option; they are often situated in peaceful spots near major cities. Some rent out rooms or cabins at reasonable rates to individuals and families— especially during slow times. Church camps are the ideal place to detox; many offer onsite food service and recreation facilities, and there are chapels and trails to facilitate contemplation, prayer, and journaling. Most camps welcome guests irrespective of their religious beliefs.

Once you've begun your detox, prepare to experience withdrawals. Damon Zahariades writes:

> Giving up your phone, tablet, video game console, and internet access is going to be a shock to your system. Your brain has become accustomed to the dopamine rush it experiences whenever you feed your addiction. It won't want to forfeit that sensation. Expect your brain to revolt, triggering intense cravings for the things you've temporarily given up.[1]

Don't thrust yourself into a detox with nothing but walls or trees to stare at. Take a paperback novel, a pair of knitting needles, a sketch book, or a deck of cards along. Practice a favorite hobby. If you're camping, plan to rent a canoe for the afternoon. Don't let yourself get too bored or you're more likely to relapse.

Detoxing with a friend is a great way to stay on the straight and narrow, but make sure your friend goes tech free too. Good conversation is a healthy way to stimulate your brain. And if one of you is tempted to stray, the other can provide encouragement and accountability.

You can do a detox without leaving home, but it's more of a challenge. People tend to associate activities with places. For instance, plopping down onto your familiar couch may tell your brain it's time to play video games or watch a movie. Sitting at the breakfast table may trigger an intense desire to check social media. However, detoxing at home does have one big advantage: you can create new associations that will help you resist temptation after your detox is complete.

Detoxing at home requires more preparation to make your environment device-free. Give your phone, tablet, and laptop to a friend. And while you're at it, disable your TV, game console, and Wi-Fi router by removing the power cords. Hand those to your friend too.

Rather than sit at home staring at all your disabled devices, plan real-life activities while you're detoxing. Dates with friends and family, getting outdoors, and hobbies top the list. It's the perfect time to dine out, visit that museum you've been wishing to see, or take a drive in the country. Biking is one of my favorite detox activities. Be sure to put these activities on a list or a schedule, because what you schedule is what you do.

One the most beneficial things you can do during a detox is to practice chatting with strangers. Here's a tip: the easiest way to start a conversation is to smile and ask them something about themselves.

Good conversationalists listen intently and ask gently probing questions based on what they hear. "You're from Galveston? How do you like living so close to the beach?"

Journaling can be tremendously helpful during a detox. When you experience withdrawal, pour your struggles out via pen and paper: *"11:00 a.m. Saturday—I'm three hours into my detox, and I feel like my head is going to explode. I've reached for my phone at least a dozen times. But I'm already beginning to feel more in tune with the real world. Colors seem brighter. Noticing things I hadn't before."* When your detox is over, look back at your journal when you're tempted to relapse.

Now what if you can't take time off for a detox? You can continue to work or go to school and detox at the same time, but you need to be wary of your danger times. For many people, that's right when they get home, because they associate relaxation with screen time.

Tech-Free Retreats

If preparing your own detox sounds exhausting, why not sign up for a pre-built one? Tech-free retreats are led by experts in screen addiction. Not only do they help you break up with your devices, but you also acquire the tools you need to succeed once you go home. Retreats are a great way to make friends, share stories with others who struggle, and engage in stimulating and fun real-life activities.

California is the epicenter of the growing tech-free retreat industry. Well-heeled guests pay upwards of nine hundred dollars a night to attend what amounts to a New Age sleepover camp complete with massage, yoga, feather beds, chakras, horse-hugging, meditation exercises, and—of course—plenty of scented candles. If you're looking for something a little less woo-woo and a lot more affordable, I keep a list of Murrow-recommended retreats at my website: www.DavidMurrow.com/screens/support. I conduct retreats myself, and I'd love to meet you at one someday.

Identify Root Causes through Therapy and Counseling

For many people, screen addiction is an external manifestation of an internal psychological wound. They bury themselves in screens:

- To drown out painful memories of the past
- To push back feelings of anxiety and fear
- As a stress reliever
- To evade difficult tasks or interpersonal interactions
- Because they've labeled themselves introverts so they can avoid people
- Because they hate solitude

Yep, a lot of people hate solitude. In fact, we've known this since 1654, when philosopher Blaise Pascal wrote, "All of humanity's problems stem from man's inability to sit quietly in a room alone."

Three hundred and sixty years later, researchers from the University of Virginia proved Pascal right.[2] They seated men and women alone in a featureless room for just twelve minutes. The subjects had nothing to do except press a button that administered an electric shock. They were given a sample shock at the beginning of the experiment, so they knew it was quite painful. Even so, 70 percent of men and 25 percent of women chose to zap themselves rather than sit quietly alone.

Picking up your smartphone or turning on the TV is simply a less painful version of the electric shock. Our devices save us from the horror of having to sit quietly with our own thoughts.

Why are we so afraid of peace, quiet, and solitude? It's those voices we hear in our heads. Many people are self-condemners. While alone, they tend to entertain negative thoughts about themselves. Others hear condemning words that were spoken against them years ago:

- "You'll never amount to anything."
- "You're a failure."
- "Why can't you be more like your sister?"
- "Nobody would want to be with you."
- "I wish you'd never been born."

Screen entertainment is a quick way to quiet these condemning voices. Screens distract us from our pain, but the underlying wound remains.

If any of these voices sounds familiar to you, I would highly recommend the services of a professional counselor who practices cognitive behavioral therapy. A few visits to a counselor helped me deal with the legacy of an angry and controlling father. I emerged a better man, much more comfortable in my own skin, able to enjoy living in the moment, and far less prone to zoning out in front of my computer or TV. My wife will testify that I'm a more patient and loving man for having gone through counseling.

Many men scoff at the idea of therapy. I refused to see a counselor for years. I didn't see the need. I was just fine—everybody else was messed up. Besides, I saw no value in sitting on a couch and telling some woman about my feelings.

But after my family confronted me about my screen obsessions and my darkening mood, I gave in. I scheduled an appointment with a counselor named Ernie, a tough old bird with whom I shared a common faith.

Our first session was incredibly awkward. Ernie began asking me questions. I was evasive. I didn't want to let him in. Then he told me a story I've never forgotten. It was a parable:

A boy was imprisoned in a cave by a fierce dragon. As long as the boy stayed in the cave, he was safe, but if he tried to escape, the dragon would turn and breathe fire at him. Years passed, and the boy became a man. Eventually, the dragon died, but the man had forgotten the way out of the cave. He remained imprisoned the rest of his life and died alone.

Ernie explained the parable to me: All of us are burned by dragons as children and young adults. The dragon might be a parent, a bully, or some other heartless person. We learn ways of coping with our pain through a compulsion or addiction; that's our cave. We end up living in darkness, and that darkness spills over onto the people we love.

Ernie looked at me and said, "My job was to help you identify your dragon, prove that it's dead, and then show you the way out of the cave. Now, are you coming with me?"

Men, therapy isn't sitting on a couch talking to a woman about your feelings. It's dragon-slaying. Make the courageous decision to stop living in darkness and isolation—if not for yourself, then for the people you love and care about.

The Spiritual Path to Freedom

The Christian church has been helping addicts find freedom for almost two thousand years. The path to redemption is a simple one with just three steps: *Repentance. Confession. Accountability.*

The word *repentance* sounds old-fashioned and religious, but it's actually a navigational term. *Repent* simply means "turn around." In other words, recognize and admit you are going the wrong way. Stop living in denial and be honest about your compulsions. Until you decide you want to be free, you won't be.

The second step is confession. Find a trusted confidant and tell them what you've been doing. Confession is an act of humility that's strangely out of sync with our modern, blame-the-other-person mentality. It's one of the most difficult things you'll ever attempt. You will be petrified in the hours leading up to your confession. Your brain will think of a million excuses to cancel the meeting, lie to your confessor, or minimize your transgressions. But the moment you open your mouth, you'll begin to experience peace. When your confession is complete, your heart will feel lighter than it's been in years. Confession is like going to the gym—it hurts while you're doing it, but you'll love the results.

Please—don't confess online. Do it face-to-face. Confess with your mouth to a friend, a professional counselor, or a small group of trusted confidants.

And don't forget accountability. Once you've confessed, ask your confessor to hold you accountable. Check in regularly face-to-face or via chat. If you're struggling, be honest. If you're winning, be glad.

Many churches offer accountability groups for people dealing with various addictions and compulsions. If you're looking for a small-group experience that specifically addresses screen addictions (particularly sexual ones), some large churches offer men's Conquer Series groups from a professionally produced video curriculum that explains the roots of sexual compulsions using brain science. Many churches also offer Celebrate Recovery groups for people who struggle with hurt, pain, or addiction of any kind. The nice thing about church-based groups is they're almost always free.

If you have neglected or abused others as a result of your screen addiction, you may benefit from a twelve-step group. A growing number focus specifically on tech addictions. I keep updated links to all these resources on my website: www.DavidMurrow.com/screens/support.

Online Accountability Software

Pete the porn user hates his compulsion but feels powerless against it. Each time he looks at porn, he feels shame, which leads to isolation. Then a trigger comes along. Stress at work, a fight with his wife, or an unexpected expense. And where does he turn for relief? More porn, which gives him momentary relief by flooding his brain with dopamine. The moment the dopamine wears off, he feels more shame, which causes him to isolate, and the cycle begins again.

Modern accountability software breaks this cycle. Pete installs monitoring software on all his devices and then recruits a buddy to keep him accountable. If he tries to uninstall or defeat the software, his buddy gets a report. Meanwhile, artificial intelligence takes random screenshots and examines them for inappropriate content. Pete's buddy gets a confidential report anytime Pete slips up. His buddy is there to offer encouragement and a gentle kick in the pants. Just knowing his ally will see the report gives Pete the power to resist porn. His shame subsides, and he no longer feels isolated.

There are a number of other online accountability tools that can help you beat porn. I keep a current list and links at my website: www. DavidMurrow.com/screens/support.

Inpatient Addiction Treatment

A self-administered digital detox may not work for individuals with severe screen addictions. Fortunately, inpatient screen addiction treatment options are now available.

China was the first nation to recognize video game addiction as a clinical disorder. As many as twenty-four million Chinese youths have been diagnosed, and the nation has built a network of boot-camp style recovery centers. They use a tough love approach and claim a 75 percent success rate in helping screen-addled young men kick their gaming habits.

In the United States, one of the pioneers in the field is reSTART, which specializes in helping severely addicted young men in the grip of video gaming and porn addictions. A team of mental health professionals lives and works with these men at a retreat center ten miles southeast of Redmond, Washington. These Addicted Alberts stay anywhere from a week to three months in a large communal cabin. They receive intense daily therapy while doing chores, developing real life skills, and reacclimating their brains to the real world.

If you or someone you love is in the grips of severe screen addiction, please refer to the list of treatment centers at my website: www.DavidMurrow.com/screens/support.

I Want to Help Others with Their Screen Use

4.1

I'm a Parent Who Wants to Help My Kids

In *The Lord of the Rings* trilogy, Frodo the hobbit possesses a magic ring that makes him invisible. But that invisibility comes at a price. Each time Frodo slips the ring onto his finger, he is transported into a shadowy netherworld where he becomes visible to Sauron, the ring's wicked creator. The pitiful creature Gollum, one of the ring's previous custodians, wore it often and was completely controlled and corrupted by Sauron's dark powers.

As a modern parent, you too have been given a magic ring. Screens can make your child's crying, nagging, and boredom disappear instantly. She becomes invisible, which can be handy when you're traveling, shopping, or just need a few minutes to get things done.

But that invisibility comes at a price. The more your child turns to screens to be soothed, entertained, or distracted, the more she falls under their power. She is transported into an artificial netherworld, removed from the challenges of real life. At the same time, she becomes visible to advertisers who want her money, extremists who want her mind, and predators who want her body.

Children are particularly vulnerable to the influence of screens. Their brains are still forming. They're developing habits that will follow them the rest of their lives. A child who never learns to regulate his emotions without the help of a screen will have a hard time doing so in adulthood. Many parents have watched in horror as their once healthy, happy kids become screen-obsessed Gollums—harsh, angry, moody, and obsessed with their *precioussss* screens. And many parents feel powerless against the sewer pipe of unhealthy content the screen world gushes toward their children.

Perhaps you've heard of Steve Jobs, the legendary co-founder of Apple Inc. Before he passed away from pancreatic cancer in 2012, journalist Nick Bilton asked him how much his kids used the iPad. To Bilton's surprise, Jobs told him they'd never used one. "We limit how much technology our kids use in the home," Jobs said. Bill Gates, the co-founder of Microsoft, "implemented a cap on screen time when his daughter started developing an unhealthy attachment to a video game. He also didn't let his kids get cell phones until they turned fourteen."[1] In Silicon Valley, low-tech, screen-free Waldorf schools are booming in popularity, educating the children of tech millionaires by using pencils and paper.[2]

So if tech innovators are keeping a tight leash on their own children's screen time, perhaps parents would be wise to follow their example. Here's how.

Make a Plan. Start Early. Stick with It.

Here's best piece of advice I can give parents:

- Write up a screen-use plan for your kids
- Implement it at birth
- Stick with it

Here's why it's important to start early: once your kids start putting the golden ring of screen time on their fingers, it's very hard to get it off. Many parents who have tried to limit their children's screen time after the fact tell stories of how their kids had meltdowns, flew into a rage, or even ran away from home. It's much easier to enforce limits from the time they're young.

Some parents are giving preschoolers their own tablets as entertainment devices. This is an extraordinarily bad idea. "But it's not connected to the internet, and we've got the parental controls locked down," you say. Fine. But what about the precedent you're setting? Your child has her own device that she can control and access at age three. What do you plan to tell her when she's eight and wants her own mobile phone? Not to mention the fact that she's training her brain to seek screen novelty any time she's bored.

Parents sometimes stray from the plan in a moment of weakness. Kids play one parent against the other. Hold firm to the plan and you'll greatly lessen the odds your children will become captive to their screens. I keep a screen use plan for parents at my website: www. DavidMurrow.com/screens/tools.

Preschoolers and Grade-Schoolers

What's the absolute best way your preschooler can spend her time? According to three decades of research, free, "unstructured, un-plugged play is the best way for young children to learn to think creatively, to problem solve, and to develop reasoning, communication and motor skills. Free play also teaches them how to entertain themselves."[3] This is why the American Academy of Pediatrics offers the following recommendations to parents of young children:[4]

- For children younger than eighteen months, avoid use of screen media other than video-chatting. Parents of children eighteen to twenty-four months of age who want to introduce digital media should choose high-quality programming and watch it with their children to help them understand what they're seeing.

- For children two to five years old, limit screen use to one hour per day of high-quality programs. Parents should co-view media with children to help them understand what they are seeing and apply it to the world around them.
- For children ages six and older, place consistent limits on the time spent using media—and the types of media—and make sure it does not take the place of adequate sleep, physical activity, or other behaviors essential to health.
- Designate media-free times together, such as dinner or driving, as well as media-free locations at home, such as bedrooms.
- Have ongoing communication about online citizenship and safety, including treating others with respect online and offline.

But there's one action item the AAP guidelines miss, and it's the most important one: *Parents must get their own screen use under control first.*

Actions Speak Louder

If you spend an inordinate amount of your free time absorbed in your TV, computer, video game, or smart device, your kids will grow up to do the same. Children follow their parents' examples more than their advice. Catherine Steiner-Adair writes:

We read so much about kids tuning out and living online, but that's only half of the problem. More worrisome to me are the ways in which parents are checking out of family time, disappearing themselves and offering that behavior as a model for their children.[5]

Why do parents check out? They're tired. Stressed. Lonely. They just want to unwind for five minutes and enjoy that shot of dopamine after a hard day at work. "Just five minutes" can easily turn into an hour or more.

Many kids are deeply hurt by the lack of attention they receive from their screen-besotted parents. Steiner-Adair conducts focus groups in schools across the country. "The take-home message I am hearing from children of all ages is this: They feel the disconnect. They can tell when their parents' attention is on screens or calls…it feels 'bad and sad' to be ignored. And they are tired of being the 'call waiting' in their parents' lives."[6]

This was my error. When my kids were young, I sat in the living room, absorbed in my screen, barely looking up. If I could turn back time, I'd close my laptop and give my kids a hearty grin every time I saw their precious little faces.

Parents, you must set the example:

- Resist the urge to check or use your devices in the presence of a family member. Instead, train yourself to put the device down, look them in the eye, and smile.
- If you need to take a call or answer an email, apologize and leave the room. When you return, give family members your full attention.
- Implement a "no screens at the dinner table" policy that applies to parents too.
- Eat dinner at a table so you can look each other in the eye.
- Turn the TV completely off at mealtime, even if it's in the other room. Don't just mute the sound.

- After dinner, turn the TV on only if you're planning to watch something together. Turn it off when you're done.
- Resist the urge to pull out your phone and photograph everything.

That last one is important. Parents (particularly those captivated by social media) are often tempted to snap a photo of everything they see and experience. It's only natural—when their kids do something cute, they don't want to lose the memory. But they're also hoping to win Instagram by capturing images that make good posts. They're also teaching their kids to reach for their smartphones instead of living in the moment.

The golden ring of screen time can also be used to create the illusion of family harmony. Give everyone their own screen—and instantly the house is calm. In sixty seconds, you've pacified bickering siblings and tranquilized hormonal teens.

But this artificial peace comes at a price. As each family member retreats to a corner to stream TV, play video games, or scroll through social media, they become strangers. MIT professor Sherry Turkle calls this "being alone together"—families that are physically present but who pay little attention to one another.

A healthy family dynamic emerges through hundreds of mini interactions between parents, children, and siblings over the years: a smile, a hand on a shoulder, a dad joke (groan), an argument, correction, forgiveness, and being noticed. Screen time is preempting many of these constructive daily encounters. What remains of our interactions is mostly negative or corrective: *Have you done your homework? Why is your room such a pigsty? Have you washed your soccer uniform? When are you going to fill out your college application?* Kids begin to perceive their parents as joyless nags who exist only to correct their missteps or keep them on schedule.

Some parents go too far in the other direction, using screens to avoid upsetting conversations about homework, chores, and the like.

The home descends into chaos as issues are never addressed. On top of this, kids learn that conflict avoidance via screen is easier than negotiating the give-and-take of real-life relationships.

Device Ownership and Control

It's very important that your kids know they may not access screen content without your permission. Tell them plainly: "Every screen in the house belongs to your parents and remains under our control."

- Prohibit kids from picking up a mobile device or turning on the TV without your permission. This rule applies until they are given their own devices as teens. Tell them: "It's not your TV, your tablet, or your smartphone. You may not access any screen without parental permission."
- "No screens in bedrooms. This applies as long as you are under our roof."
- Video games: ban headsets and disable text, voice, and video-chat features on your kids' console. Let them compete against other people in the room, not over the internet. Predators use these channels to meet and groom victims.
- TVs, video games, laptops, and handheld devices must be accessed in living rooms/kitchens/patio areas where others can see what's going on.

Have the First "Tech Talk" with Your Child around Age Eight

Even if your child doesn't have his own personal device, his friends do. That's why it's important to talk with your kids about the dangers of screen content while they're young. The average age when kids first view porn is ten for boys and eleven for girls. Many kids stumble across it when searching the internet for something else. Once they see porn, they often begin seeking it out of curiosity, as early as six years of age. Help your child understand:

- "Don't believe everything you see on a screen."
- "Sometimes you'll see naked people on a screen. These things are fake. They are placed there by people who are lying about real life."
- "There are bad people in the world who may try to contact you through a screen. Do not talk to strangers online."
- "If you ever see something on a screen that disturbs you, no matter what it is, you can always come to your parents. We won't be mad. In fact, we will take you out for a donut to thank you for being honest with us."

Having the Second "Tech Talk" with Your Young Teen

When your child reaches puberty, it's time for a second talk, and this one's going to be easy. This book contains the perfect tool to help you start the conversation: the parables.

Sit your young teen down and read the Parable of the Four Brothers, which is located in Chapter 3.1 of this book. Then ask him what he thinks the parable means. You may hear things like, "I dunno," or something completely non-screen related. That's OK. Let him come up with whatever. Don't correct him—just listen.

Then turn the page and read the explanation of the parable. Turn to him and ask this question:

"Do you know anyone who uses screens too much, like Excessive Eddie?"

That should prime the pump. Here are some good follow-up questions:

- "Do you ever feel ignored by someone who's using a screen? Do I ever make you feel that way?"
- "Do you know anybody who uses screens for harmful purposes like Dishonorable Dan?"
- "Have you ever seen hurtful or inappropriate things on screens that made you feel uncomfortable?"
- "Has anyone ever shown you pornography?"
- "What about social media or video games? Do you know any Addicted Alberts?"

When you feel like it's time to bring the conversation to a close, schedule a time to read the second parable in section one of this book (the fishbowl). If you want to make a huge impact on your child, gather the props. Let him fill the fishbowl (or any similar container) with water. Watch together as the ping pong balls drown and pop out the top. Then talk to him about brain capacity and the things he thinks about.

Before you read the second parable, sit down and watch the *The Matrix* together, if you think the movie is appropriate. Then talk about the nature of reality, illusion, and discernment.

You may want to read the final two parables from the life of David in one sitting. Explain how "wolves" overstimulate our brains, then segue into the Parable of the Kingdom. Your teen needs to understand how isolating and destructive a digital kingdom can be. Again, there are great follow-up questions:

- "Do you know any digital kings or queens?"
- "Do you ever enjoy screen life more than real life?"

- "Why do you think people spend so much time on screens? Is it really like locking themselves behind castle walls?"
- "Why is it important to learn to deal with difficult people?"
- "Why is it important not to fill your mind with harmful content and ideas?"

As your teen matures, you can use these parables as a quick way of correcting or connecting:

- "Hey, come out of your digital castle. The real world is calling!"
- "This article is just a wolf that is trying to upset you and get your attention."
- "Give your fishbowl a rest and go outside."

Behold the power of a parable. Two people who both know its meaning can say a lot with a few words. I've got a discussion guide based on the parables that you can download at my website: www.DavidMurrow.com/screens/HowTo.

Once you've briefed your kids on the hazards of the screen world, they may be ready for their own phones. Here's some device advice:

Personal Devices and Teens

- Do not give your kids a personal device until eighth grade at the earliest. If you want to stay in touch, give them an old-fashioned flip phone or a limited feature phone that does not have access to the internet. Believe it or not, flip phones are becoming cool again. There are new options all the time, so I keep an updated list of these devices at my website: www.DavidMurrow.com/screens/families.

- Remind them: as the owner of every device, *you* have unlimited access any time of the day or night. In addition, you keep all passwords to all their apps. Let your kids know you will be checking their phones regularly to keep them safe.

- As the owner of the phone, you control which apps can be installed.

- Do not install apps that allow disappearing posts, such as Snapchat.

- No video-streaming apps (YouTube, Hulu, Netflix, Prime, etc.). If they want to stream a movie, they can do it at home in the living room with your permission.

- Set up a central charging station in your bedroom. The phones must be on their charging cradles by a certain time (before dinner, for example). If your kids touch their devices without permission, they lose them for a week.

What If the Situation Is Already Out of Control?

What if your kids are eleven and nine and they've never had meaningful limits on screen time? If you decide to impose limits, you can expect titanic resistance. Stand firm.

The best strategy is substitution. Take the video game console away but put something else in its place—sports, music lessons, an after-school basketball program—anything to absorb that youthful energy and get your kids back into the real world. Reading before bedtime as a family was something my kids always looked forward to.

One of the most difficult situations emerges in joint-custody situations where one parent is indulgent and the other is strict. Kids are whipsawed between a household with limitless screen time and another with strict boundaries. Do whatever you can to get on the same page with your ex.

Filtering and Monitoring

If all this monitoring seems like a part-time job, you're right. You need help. Fortunately, the same screens that vex you can also make monitoring much easier.

Television: Modern TVs, cable, and satellite set-top boxes have parental controls that block shows by rating, so your kids won't accidentally tune into a program with inappropriate content. But you must activate the controls. Smart TVs can also lock kids out of all apps or set limits within each app. (Netflix allows parents to lock kids out of adult content, for example.) Also, some streaming platforms offer separate family-friendly apps for smart TVs.

Control hardware: Parental-control devices plug into a home Wi-Fi router, allowing parents to control kids' access and filter content all from a single app that resides on the parents' phones. Adults can set bedtimes or time limits and control access to selected sites and content. They can even reward kids with a little extra screen time when chores are done (not sure that's such a good idea, but the option is there).

Monitoring services: Several companies offer to monitor the traffic on your child's devices for adult content, signs of depression or self-harm, predatory messages, or cyberbullying. Parents get an alert whenever potential problems arise. These services even suggest ways parents can start an age-appropriate conversation if kids are exposed to harmful content.

For a complete list of the latest and greatest filtering and monitoring tools, visit my website: www.DavidMurrow.com/screens/families.

4.2

I Want to Help a Friend or Spouse

Excessive Eddies, Dishonorable Dans, and Addicted Alberts are often in denial about their screen use. They're so accustomed to living inside their digital kingdoms that they cannot see how abnormal and out-of-control their lives have become.

As a trusted friend or spouse, you're in a unique position to help them see the truth. Before you take any action, I'd encourage you to pray specifically for your loved one's deliverance. You're going to need all the help (both earthly and heavenly) you can get.

If the problem is severe, Al may need professional help—a move many addicts resist. You may want to gather some of Addicted Albert's friends for an intervention. Just sit everyone down and address Albert's screen use directly. Be gentle and encouraging. Let Al know you're concerned about him and you're willing to do whatever it takes to help.

If a group intervention isn't possible, a one-on-one conversation can spark change. Here are some ways to bring up the subject:

How to Talk to a Screen-Obsessed Friend

It's important to avoid inflammatory statements like:

"Al, why are you so addicted to TV?"

"Al, you know you're screwing up your life by spending all your time on that stupid game."

Accusations will put Al on the defensive. Instead, be humble. One of the best ways to start a conversation is to tell your story:

"Al, did you know I used to play video games about six hours a day?"

If you don't have a story, try a gentle opener like this:

"Al, what's the longest you've ever played video games in one sitting? Have you ever gone all night?

The goal is to get Al to tell his own story. The more Al talks about his situation, the more likely he is to admit his obsession. So ask questions. Once Al fesses up, be sure to share one of your own struggles to show you can relate. Try something like this:

"Man, I can relate. My screen addiction is binge-watching TV series."

See how you've placed yourself on Al's level? He will feel a lot less lectured or controlled if you admit to struggling yourself. Now it's time to ask Al how he feels about his screen use:

"Have you ever felt the need to cut back on your gaming?"

If Al says, *"Nah, I'm good,"* then go back to your own story:

"I used to feel that way, but I didn't realize what I was missing. I'm a lot happier now that I've got my gaming under control."

This is the moment of truth. Either Al shuts you down, or he leaves an opening. If he seems interested at all, go ahead and ask the question:

"I figured out how to cut back on my screen use, and if you're interested, I can show you how."

If you're close friends, you might suggest doing a joint digital detox. Once again, the key is humility. Make sure Al understands you're trying to help, not judge.

One more thing: there's an absolute zero percent chance your conversation will go exactly the way I laid it out. Be ready to improvise. Ask God to give you the words you need as you need them. Communicate concern—not condemnation—every step of the way.

Don't be surprised if Al greets your overtures with denial, sarcasm, or hostility. You're asking Gollum to hand over his precious ring. Expect a few flashes of snarling anger, but don't take it personally. The initial conversation may not end well, but once Al cools down, he may come back and admit his weakness. Your job is to plant the seed. Then wait patiently for the harvest.

How to Talk to a Spouse about Her Screen Time

How do you talk to your beloved about her screen use? You may be able to address it with a lighthearted conversation. Just be honest:

"Hey, sometimes I think you love your phone more than me. How about you pay me a little attention?"

If your spouse takes this well, tell her this is an ongoing issue. She may be totally unaware that she's locking herself away in her digital castle. Agree on a code word to alert your spouse whenever she slips up:

"Honey, you're in your castle again…"

You might try using a little humor. When I get out of balance, my wife says, "David, how is your silver mistress today?" She's referring to the shiny MacBook Pro, my beloved laptop. When I hear these words, I smile, close the lid, and give her my attention.

If your spouse is the type to respond to soft incentives, try something fun like this:

"Let's make a deal. If you're screen-free after dinner until bedtime, you get a back massage."

"You know, honey, it's very sexy when you put down your video game controller and give me your full attention—if you know what I mean."

Now if your spouse is the prickly type or heavily addicted, this can be a much thornier conversation. Timing is everything. Don't initiate the conversation when she's absorbed in her device or she may interpret your effort to help as an attack. Have the conversation face-to-face so you can show empathy.

Again, DO NOT start with an accusation such as this:

"You know, your stupid Instagram obsession is ruining our relationship." And definitely don't say, *"Are you using that iPad to avoid me? Checking out old boyfriends or something?"*

Instead, affirm your love for her:

"Honey, this may sound silly, but sometimes I feel like I'm second to Instagram in your life."

"I get frustrated when I'm talking to you, but you're absorbed in social media. It's not just me; the kids are feeling the distance too."

Hopefully, that will start a conversation. If she admits her obsession, be prepared to suggest a digital detox or a concrete strategy for cutting back. A good starting point: read this book's parables together and come to a mutual understanding of what screens do to us.

However, your spouse may become defensive, particularly if there's already tension in the relationship. She may respond with anger:

"It's just a few minutes in the evening. Lay off."

Resist the urge to fire back. Remember, a soft answer turns away wrath.

"I know you deserve a break. But I'm concerned about our family. We're not communicating like we used to."

She may seek to justify her obsession by accusing you of being a hypocrite, like this:

"MY Instagram? What about your video gaming?"

"I'm not the one who got caught looking at porn a few years ago!"

These barbs may hurt, but you must resist the urge to fight back. This is where the battle is won or lost. DO NOT justify your behavior. Instead, apologize. You win by losing:

"Honey, I'm sorry. I had no idea my gaming bothered you so much."

"Yeah, I know I used to do porn, and I'm really sorry. I hate that about myself."

Then be quiet. Unless you're married to a complete sociopath, your spouse should respond with contrition. Move the conversation forward, maintaining a posture of love and humility. Be patient.

Once your spouse accepts the fact that something needs to change, it's time to suggest a solution:

"I've been thinking about this, and I believe we'd both benefit from doing a digital detox together. What do you think?"

Once again, I can guarantee the actual conversation will take unexpected twists and turns. But it's worth the risk. One of the kindest things my wife does for me is tell me the truth when I'm running off the rails. I do the same for her. Over the years, we've both learned to accept correction from each other without becoming defensive.

I have more resources at my website, including videos that demonstrate how to talk to someone you love about their screen obsessions: www.DavidMurrow.com/screens/HowTo.

4.3

I'm a Teacher Who Wants to Help My Students

"**W**e must bridge the Digital Divide."

"Digital equity—the civil rights issue of our time."

"Computers in the classroom will help our children compete in the technology-driven future. We can't fall behind other nations."

"Pew Research reports nearly one in five teens can't always finish their homework because of the digital divide."

Politicians, tech companies, and school administrators have issued declarations like these for decades, pleading for funding to expand children's access to computers and broadband internet. Atlanta Public Schools is spending millions of dollars to give every sixth- and seventh-grader a laptop. The Los Angeles Unified School District has already spent an eye-popping $1.3 billion to issue every student a tablet computer. Public schools in Baltimore County, Maryland, began going all-digital in 2014 to the point of eliminating paper and pencils in many classrooms.

Five years later, many parents were clamoring to bring the paper and pencils back. The reason? Schools that have gone "all in" on screen-based teaching are generally seeing lower student performance, particularly on standardized tests.[1]

The need for screens in school seems obvious: technology powers the modern economy. The jobs of the future will require computer skills, so it makes sense to start kids on these high-tech tools early, right?

Wrong. Kids can easily get all the computer skills they'll need in high school—even those students who eventually go into fields like computer programming. There's absolutely no reason to give every child an internet-connected device in grade school or even middle school.

Our political leaders are digital Pollyannas, touting the benefits of universal screen use and web access while ignoring its perils. The same broadband connection that enables kids to do their homework can also expose them to predators, cyberbullying, and corrosive content. It immobilizes their bodies and can lead to a host of negative health outcomes. Students already spend most of their free time gawking at their screens, and now screens are coming to dominate classroom time as well. All this screen time is turning our teens into hyper-distractible couch potatoes who have trouble concentrating. Catherine Steiner-Adair writes:

> A brilliant, beloved high school teacher, Steven Fine, tells me about the growing number of students for whom even the most engaged, creative teaching "just can't hold their attention."[2]

Diane Birdwell, a twenty-year veteran teacher from Texas, stopped using screen-based teaching when she began noticing a growing digital dependency. "It has hampered their ability to think on their own," Birdwell told the *Wall Street Journal*. "They don't know how to calculate basic math functions in their minds. They are being mentally crippled by these things."[3]

Screens in School: Helpful or Harmful to Learning?

Computer labs began showing up in high schools in the 1970s and in elementary schools a decade later. So what have we learned in the ensuing years? Are computers the essential learning tools tech boosters led us to believe they were?

A massive study of student achievement in thirty nations found that frequent in-school computer use is associated with lower test scores. The best-performing schools allow computers, but in low to moderate doses. According to Helen Lee Bouygues, president of the Paris-based Reboot Foundation:

> When students report having access to classroom computers and using these devices on an infrequent basis, they show better performance.... But when students report using these devices every day, and for several hours during the school day, performance lowers dramatically.
>
> Across most countries, a low to moderate use of school technology was generally associated with better performance, relative to students reporting no computer use at all.... But students who reported a high use of school technology trailed behind peers who reported moderate use.[4]

Schools should employ screens for specific tasks where computers are indispensable. For example, computerized spreadsheets are a must for accounting students. Aspiring engineers must learn to use CAD software. Translation software helps non-English speakers catch up to their peers. Even young kids can create engaging PowerPoint presentations to supplement a written report.

But when screens become a primary educational delivery device throughout the day, students experience a host of negative side effects: hyperstimulation, distractibility, and irritability, as well as reduced social and physical activity. Not to mention those lower test scores.

As I mentioned in the introduction, as I am completing this book, the world is in the midst of the first wave of the COVID-19 pandemic. The schools that educate more than 90 percent of the world's students closed simultaneously, and the vast majority of instruction moved online. Although it's far too early to evaluate the impact this is having on students' learning, the teachers I've spoken to have seen a noticeable drop in student engagement, particularly in the younger grades. Some of their pupils have simply disappeared. We're engaged in an enormous, real-time experiment to see if online learning can replace face-to-face classroom instruction, with our kids serving as guinea pigs.

Screens have shown a great deal of promise in educating adults. Most colleges offer online classes, and some universities exist exclusively online (in this pandemic season, almost all do). But young children still benefit greatly from having a real, flesh-and-blood instructor to guide the learning process.

The Real Screen Problem: Smartphones

The larger concern for many teachers isn't school-issued computers; it's the devices kids bring to school themselves. Mobile phone use has become the top disciplinary issue in many high schools, causing enormous friction between students and staff. Their constant ringing, chirping, and buzzing keep pupils from concentrating in class. Kids who are buried in their phones don't socialize as much and are more prone to anxiety and loneliness. Phones can be fought over, stolen, or hacked. They enable cheating on exams. Kids bully one another by shooting embarrassing photos and videos at school and posting them to social media. And because they're connected to the internet, phones can bring unwelcome content onto school grounds.

Schools have a variety of policies for dealing with smartphones. Here are a few:

Outright Bans

The simplest way to deal with phones would be to prohibit them from being brought to school. Such a policy is fairly easy to implement in elementary school, but a blanket ban is impractical in the upper grades. High schoolers need their devices after the final bell rings. And many parents insist on 24/7 connectivity with their teens. Indeed, parents are among the worst offenders when it comes to texting their kids during the school day.

Nevertheless, some school districts do not allow students to carry phones. In 2018, the entire nation of France banned children under the age of fifteen from taking mobile devices to school. On the other hand, New York City schools repealed their mobile phone ban in 2015. The blanket prohibition was difficult to enforce and proved unpopular with parents who wanted to stay in touch with their kids.

Bell-to-Bell Confinement

Many schools allow kids to keep their phones, but the devices must be locked up during classroom hours. When students enter City on a Hill Charter School in Boston, every phone is placed in an individual locking pouch. The student maintains possession of her pouched phone, but she is unable to access its functions. The pouches are unlocked at the end of the day. San Lorenzo High School in California also began using pouches in 2019. Teachers noticed an immediate change in the school's learning and social environment, with students more engaged in class and interacting more with friends during breaks and lunch.

However, videos keep popping up on YouTube teaching students how to defeat the pouches, so their effectiveness is questionable. That's one reason Brooklyn Academy of Science and the Environment (BASE) ditched its pouches in favor of a low-tech solution: volunteers collect phones each morning, sorting them into plastic bins that are delivered to each student's final class. This solution not only minimizes distraction, but it also keeps kids from skipping their last period.

Twelve Corners Middle School in Rochester, New York, has a simpler solution: students are required to keep phones in their lockers during the entire school day. Any mobile device spotted outside of a locker is subject to confiscation.

Carry but Can't Use

Burgess Hill Girls school in the United Kingdom allows students to carry phones, but they must remain off or silent and completely out of view. Jefferson Middle School in Merritt Island, Florida, requires students to complete a mobile-device contract. The phone must be turned off during the school day, including school bus time. Corte Madera Middle School in Portola Valley, California, requires phones to be off and stowed either in a locker or backpack, not in clothing or pockets.

Allowed to Use at Lunch and Passing Times

High school students in Marshall, Minnesota, are allowed to use mobiles between classes and during lunch time, but they must stow the devices during class unless the teacher authorizes in-class usage. Principal Brian Jones said the previous policy of a bell-to-bell ban on phone use was causing students unnecessary anxiety, comparing it to the comic-strip character Linus panicking when he's separated from his security blanket.[5]

Teacher's Choice

Some high schools let individual teachers decide how to handle smartphones. Josh Paley is a high school teacher in Palo Alto, California, in the heart of Silicon Valley. He requires students to stow their mobile devices in numbered pouches before class begins. In Teena Calkin's Criminal Justice and Law Enforcement class at King Tech High School in Anchorage, Alaska, students' phones "go to jail" during class—an alarmed strong box that emits an ear-piercing wail if anyone attempts a jailbreak. When class is over, the phones are released on parole.

Integrate Phones into Lessons

Veteran high school teacher Ken Halla got tired of telling his students to put their devices away, so he decided to incorporate them into his curriculum. Instead of standing at the front lecturing, Halla roams the classroom, helping students with their work. Students read material, watch subject-matter videos, and take test-prep quizzes on their phones. Halla has identified a number of useful apps that keep kids engaged in their work instead of social media. He even allows pupils to listen to music streamed off their phones while they work, provided they use headphones and keep the volume down. When class is over, his students get electronic reminders to complete homework assignments or to study for upcoming tests.[6]

Phones in College

Even college instructors are beginning to regulate their students' use of mobile phones. Lee University English professor Kevin Brown has noticed that students who are absorbed in their phones during class often fall behind. Brown may be onto something: a 2017 study found that the presence of smartphones in college lectures divides students' attention, which reduced their ability to retain what they've learned, which in turn results in lower scores on exams.[7] So in 2019, Brown began asking every student to place their phones and smartwatches in a numbered slot at the front of the lecture hall to minimize distractions. To his delight, most of his students seemed to welcome the policy.

There's No Perfect Smartphone Policy

Total phone bans are hard to enforce and create animosity between students and staff. Partial bans seem reasonable, but they also create disciplinary problems. Students get around bans by turning in "dummy" phones at the beginning of class while keeping their real devices with them. Wall pouches buzz during class; some teachers call it "the beehive." Hyper-connected parents want to be able to text their kids during school and view their location on a map.

The best way to handle phones in school is to establish a policy from day one and not deviate from it. Some kids will always push the envelope, but most appreciate and respect boundaries.

Regarding computers in class, use them as a tool for imparting specific skills—not as a teacher's assistant or babysitter.

As a teacher, you are not merely a fact-dispensing machine. You're preparing your students for adulthood. They need your support in learning to deal with relationships, conflict, and disappointment. Help them detach from their screens as much as possible. You're one of a diminishing number of grownups who has daily, face-to-face interactions with the youngsters in your care. A computer can impart information, but only you can give your pupils attention, grit, and love.

4.4

I'm a Minister Who Wants to Help My Flock

A friend of mine named Bryan (name changed) works as a youth pastor at a large church. "It's a huge battle every time we ask the students to put their phones away," he said. "People over thirty-five like you and me tend to see real life as primary and screen life as secondary. But many of our teens have the exact opposite perspective: their true life is lived on their phones. What you and I would call the real world is an unwelcome intrusion that stresses them out."

Increasingly, the eyes of churchgoers both young and old are fixed not on Jesus, but on their screens. With the average American spending nine hours a day staring at them, screens may be rightly identified as the true objects of our worship. They are absorbing the time Christians used to devote to spiritual disciplines such as prayer, meditation, fellowship, service, and thanksgiving. In exchange, our screens have given us fear, anxiety, loneliness, and a puffed-up sense of our own rightness.

The Apostle Paul commands the saints to "pray without ceasing." But that's impossible when we're filling every free moment with screen time. Enchanted by our devices, we miss opportunities to pray for or encourage people. We simply don't see them.

As our constant companions, screens are discipling us. When we need advice, we no longer seek the ancient wisdom embedded in the scriptures. Nor do we seek the godly counsel of mature Christians. Instead, we present our requests to a search engine. David Kinnaman and Mark Matlock write:

> Many of us today turn to our devices to help us make sense of the world. Young people, especially, use the screens in their pockets as counselors, entertainers, instructors, even sex educators. Why build up the courage to have what will likely be an awkward conversation with a parent, pastor, or teacher when you can just ask your phone and no one else will be the wiser?[1]

Because search engines rank pages based on popularity, the person who turns to the web for advice is more likely to encounter fashionable misinformation than timeless wisdom. The screen world prefers the trendy over the time-tested and the clanging cymbal over the still, small voice.

As screen content amplifies our sense of autonomy and affirms our individuality, adults and teens are becoming alienated from and distrustful of institutions and traditions that once gave meaning to life—including the church. Apostates who might have quietly slipped out of the pews in times past are now taking to social media to publicly announce the *deconstruction* of their faith, encouraging others to do the same. Ian Harber writes:

> The Christian tradition I grew up in—for all the wonderful things it gave me—was not prepared for a generation of

kids with access to high-speed internet. Not that the
critiques of the Bible we discovered online were new, but
they were now at the fingertips of curious folks who grew
up in evangelical bubbles. Like me. The answers given in
church seemed shallow compared to the legitimate critiques
that were a Google search or YouTube video away.[2]

The rapid-fire way we scroll through social media makes it a petri
dish for cynicism and disbelief. "Gotcha" questions are brief and
shareable: How could a loving God allow suffering? Try answering
that one on Twitter using just 280 characters. Theology and apologet-
ics require patience and deep thinking—skills that are passing away,
thanks to our screen-shortened attention spans.

As the wreckage of our digital obsessions begins washing up in
the church, parishioners will be looking to pastors and teachers for
guidance they can trust. The demand for sermons, workshops, and
individual counseling around issues of technology will grow exponen-
tially in the years to come.

As a teacher in the church, it's a struggle to know how much detail
to include in your message. There's so much depraved content on the
web. How do you warn against its dangers without exposing people
to things that can harm them? If you prescribe mutual confession
(James 5:16), what happens if a parishioner confesses to having viewed
child pornography? In twenty-six states, you'd be legally obligated to
turn the penitent over to law enforcement, even if the offense took
place years ago.

Obviously, the Bible has nothing to say about today's technology.
So how can you apply its ancient precepts to such a modern-day
challenge? How do you instruct and warn your flock about the dangers
screens pose without coming across as an alarmist? Here is a list of
twelve possible jumping-off points for your next talk, lesson, or sermon:

1. Use This Book's Parables, If You'd Like

I based this book on six parables (five at the beginning of Section I and a sixth in Chapter 3.1), and you're welcome to use any or all of them as instructional tools. David's journey from shepherd boy to king represents our lives before and after the advent of screens. Preach and teach the parallels. Be sure to emphasize how digital lordship rots our souls.

If you'd like to perform the fishbowl demonstration live (Parable #2), feel free to do so, but please acknowledge this book as your source. I have a video on my website that tells you what props you'll need to gather and how to make sure the balls come floating out the top when you add water: www.DavidMurrow.com/screens/HowTo.

2. Idolatry

The first commandment is this: *You shall have no other Gods before me.* Westerners now spend the vast majority of their free time interacting with screens. Not God. Not people. Screens are the object of our worship.

Everyone will stand before God to give an account for his life. How will we justify spending nine hours a day staring at our screens while our mission in life goes unfulfilled? Are we all high-tech Jonahs?

3. The Danger of Distraction

Christ has a mission for every one of His followers. Time that could be invested in that redemptive work is wasted watching reruns on TV and blasting imaginary on-screen foes. Meanwhile, the real world deteriorates around us.

The Bible contains many warnings against distraction. Here are a few:

- Nehemiah 6: Nehemiah is asked to step away from the work of rebuilding the city wall, but he refuses.

- Matthew 16: Jesus's stern rebuke of Peter ("Get behind me, Satan!") when the apostle suggested Christ abandon His plan to die on the cross.
- Luke 8: The parable of the seed that grew up among thorns, choked out by the cares of this world and the deceitfulness of riches.
- Hebrews 12:1: "[L]et us lay aside every weight, and sin which clings so closely, and let us run with endurance the race that is set before us...."

4. Temptation

1 John 2:16: "For all that is in the world—the desires of the flesh and the desires of the eyes and pride of life—is not from the Father but is from the world." No single verse better describes what screens do to us. They inflame our lusts with an endless gallery of sensual images (lust of the flesh), objects and lifestyles to covet (lust of the eyes), and people to look down upon (the pride of life).

5. Fake...Not Real

The vast majority of screen content is not real. TV dramas and movies are scripted. Models are airbrushed. Even so-called reality shows are partially faked (believe me, I've worked in reality TV). Misinformation and biased news proliferate online. Individuals "image craft" and "facetune" themselves to present a perfect fantasy version of their lives online.

In Matthew 23, Jesus rebuked the Pharisees for their religious image crafting, accusing them of cleaning the outside of the cup but leaving the inside (their hearts) filthy. He compared them to whitewashed tombs that look beautiful on the outside but are full of dead bones on the inside.

6. The Foolish Exchange

In the Garden, Eve squandered humanity's innocence for a bite of the apple. Esau traded his birthright to his brother Jacob for a bowl of beans. In the wilderness, Satan offered Jesus the kingdoms of the world in exchange for His worship.

Screen life is another bad trade. Screens tempt us to give up the only two valuable things we possess (time and attention) in exchange for hours of meaningless distraction. Screen users trade contentment for envy, deep relationships for shallow online interactions, genuine intimacy for pornography, and real-life impact for meaningless video game glory.

7. Screens Amplify the Wickedness of Our Current Day

Paul foretold our present situation in his letter to Timothy: "But understand this, that in the last days there will come times of difficulty. For people will be lovers of self, lovers of money, proud, arrogant, abusive, disobedient to their parents, ungrateful, unholy, heartless, unappeasable, slanderous, without self-control, brutal, not loving good, treacherous, reckless, swollen with conceit, lovers of pleasure rather than lovers of God, having the appearance of godliness, but denying its power. Avoid such people" (2 Timothy 3:1–5).

Every one of these dysfunctions existed before screens, but never before has it been so easy to practice them. Screens can and do facilitate all of these destructive attitudes and behaviors.

8. Normalization of Depravity

Graphic violence. Nudity. Profanity. Cynicism, narcissism, and pessimism. Screens make these easy to access anytime and anywhere.

The more we watch these things, the more they seem acceptable. *Game of Thrones* would have been considered pornography forty years ago; today it's "peak television" enjoyed by many who claim to follow

Christ. We are failing to guard our hearts and minds (Proverbs 4:23), blind to the underlying spiritual battle that's raging for our souls.

9. Anxiety and Fear-Producing Machines

As I wrote in Chapter 2.8, screen content is designed to make us anxious, which is the exact opposite of God's will for his children. The most frequently repeated command in the Bible is this: do not be afraid. These were the first words the angels said in announcing the birth of Jesus. In the Sermon on the Mount (Matthew 6), Jesus says to his disciples, "And which of you by being anxious can add a single hour to his span of life?" (Matthew 6:34). The Apostle Paul tells the Philippians, "Do not be anxious about anything, but in everything by prayer and supplication with thanksgiving let your requests be made known to God" (4:6). In Matthew 10, Jesus promises His followers persecution, betrayal, and death—yet even in the face of all these trials, He commands them: do not be afraid.

10. Guard Your Eyes

Twice during the Sermon on the Mount, Jesus cautions His followers about the things they look at: "Your eye is the lamp of your body. When your eye is healthy, your whole body is full of light, but when it is bad, your body is full of darkness" (Matthew 6:22–23). He also offered this stern warning: "If your right eye causes you to sin, tear it out and throw it away. For it is better that you lose one of your members than that your whole body be thrown into hell" (Matthew 5:29).

11. Screens Stoke Interpersonal Conflict

Romans 12:18 says, "If possible, so far as it depends on you, live peaceably with all." Jesus prayed in John 17 that his disciples would be unified. Yet the internet is tearing us apart—dividing us into warring tribes, even within the church. When Christians take to social media to defend their values, they often do so with such vitriol and contempt that they come across as self-righteous jerks. Teach your flock the importance of grace and humility when they interact online.

12. Fruit of the Spirit Test

Galatians 5:22–23 says, "But the fruit of the Spirit is love, joy, peace, patience, kindness, goodness, faithfulness, gentleness, self-control; against such things there is no law."

Screen content often produces the opposite.

1 Corinthians 10:23 adds, "'All things are lawful,' but not all things are helpful. 'All things are lawful,' but not all things build up."

Screen use is certainly permissible, but does it build up? Do our screen-based activities make us kinder? More patient? Less envious? Do they build community and God's Kingdom? Or do they distract us from what's truly important?

■   ■   ■

In Luke 15, Jesus tells three stories of things that are lost: a sheep, a coin, and a son. At the end of each, there is much rejoicing when that which was lost is found. There is no punishment for the sheep that wandered away or for the son who squandered his father's fortune. Instead, all three stories end with a party.

A lot of people are lost in their screens. They know their screen activities are out of control. And they imagine God looking down from Heaven, disappointed in them for watching porn or wasting their time on Instagram and video games.

You must convince your flock that God isn't angry about their screen use. As a good Father, God stands waiting to love, guide, and forgive. He's ready to start the party.

Jesus came to bring life—in abundance. That abundant life exists in the real world. The screen world is but a cheap imitation.

How to Master Real Life

I t's opening night. The stage is set, and the cast is huddled backstage. The house lights dim, and the curtain rises. At center stage stands Thomas, the handsome leading man. As the performance gets underway, Thomas flubs some of his lines. He misses cues, stands on the wrong marks, and bumps into props. The rest of the cast scrambles to adapt, trying to cover for Thomas's mistakes, but the performance is a disaster. Everyone, from the director to the stagehand, is embarrassed.

What went wrong? Thomas skipped a bunch of rehearsals. While the rest of the cast and crew were diligently practicing, Thomas was busy doing other things. When it came time to perform, he wasn't ready.

Many of us are flubbing real life because we're not rehearsing it much. Instead, we spend the vast majority of our free time immersed in screen life. When it's time to perform in real life situations, we're poorly prepared. Our hearts are gripped with anxiety. "Adulting" frightens us. We miss opportunities and make poor decisions. The people around us scramble to adapt, trying to cover for our mistakes, but it's a disaster. Everyone's embarrassed—and we feel shame, which we soothe by diving back into our screens.

I used to act in high school plays. Rehearsals were often dull, tedious, and time-consuming. Our director was moody and cast members were often squirrely. But I attended rehearsals because when the curtain rose, I wanted to be ready. I was eager to perform my role to the best of my ability. And I didn't want to let my fellow cast members down.

Compared to screen life, real life can be dull and tedious. Work can be monotonous. Responsibilities weigh heavily. People can be moody and squirrely. But over time you learn to deal with the boredom and to play well with others. The more you rehearse together, the better everyone becomes.

I believe each person has a sacred role to play in life. Some refer to it as a mission or a calling. It's the most important thing you'll do. Your part may not be highly visible. It could be a supporting role, or you may even serve backstage. But every cast member must play his or her part, or everyone suffers.

Malcolm Gladwell says it takes ten thousand hours to truly master any skill. If you're going to master real life, you've got to get the hours in. So if you're spending 70 percent of your free time on screens and 30 percent in real life, flip the script. Invite a neighbor over. Join an organization and attend the meetings. Take up a hobby. Adopt a pet. Manage your finances. Be in the real world. And most importantly, deal with difficult things, even when you'd rather be binge-watching Netflix.

The more you rehearse real life, the better you'll have it down. The rest of the cast is counting on you. I'm confident that when your moment comes, you'll be ready.

Notes

Chapter 1.1: The Parable of Max and the Sea

1. Patrick Shanley, "Gaming Usage up 75 Percent Amid Coronavirus Outbreak, Verizon Reports," *The Hollywood Reporter*, March 17, 2020, https://www.hollywoodreporter.com/news/gaming-usage-up-75-percent-coronavirus-outbreak-verizon-reports-1285140.

2. Joshua B. Grubbs, "Porn Use Is Up, Thanks to the Pandemic," The Conversation, April 8, 2020, https://theconversation.com/porn-use-is-up-thanks-to-the-pandemic-134972.

3. Andrea Petersen, "More People Are Taking Drugs for Anxiety and Insomnia, and Doctors Are Worried," *Wall Street Journal*, May 25, 2020, https://www.wsj.com/articles/more-people-are-taking-drugs-for-anxiety-and-insomnia-and-doctors-are-worried-11590411600.

4. Gary Polakovic, "Pandemic Drives Alcohol Sales—and Raises Concerns about Substance Abuse," USC News, April 14, 2020, https://news.usc.edu/168549/covid-19-alcohol-sales-abuse-stress-relapse-usc-experts/.

5. Scott Neuman, "Global Lockdowns Resulting in 'Horrifying Surge' in Domestic Violence, U.N. Warns," National Public Radio, April 6, 2020, https://www.npr.org/sections/coronavirus-live-updates/2020/04/06/827908402/global-lockdowns-resulting-in-horrifying-surge-in-domestic-violence-u-n-warns.

6. Fernando Alfonso III, "The Pandemic Is Causing an Exponential Rise in the Online Exploitation of Children, Experts Say," CNN, May 25, 2020, https://www.cnn.com/2020/05/25/us/child-abuse-online-coronavirus-pandemic-parents-investigations-trnd/index.html.

Chapter 1.2: The Parable of the Fishbowl

1. "Who Are America's Toilet Texters?: Smartphone Bathroom Habits (Texting on the Toilet Study)," BankMyCell.com, https://www.bankmycell.com/blog/cell-phone-usage-in-toilet-survey.

Chapter 1.4: The Parable of David and the Wolf

1. Nicholas Kardaras, *Glow Kids* (New York, New York: Griffin Publishers, 2017), 20–22.
2. Victoria L. Dunckley, "Electronic Screen Syndrome: An Unrecognized Disorder?" *Psychology Today*, July 23, 2012, https://www.psychologytoday.com/us/blog/mental-wealth/201207/electronic-screen-syndrome-unrecognized-disorder.
3. Daniel J. Levitin, "Why the Modern World Is Bad for Your Brain," The Guardian, January 18, 2015, https://www.theguardian.com/science/2015/jan/18/modern-world-bad-for-brain-daniel-j-levitin-organized-mind-information-overload.

Chapter 1.5: The Parable of the Kingdom

1. Maryam Moshin, "10 Amazon Statistics You Need to Know in 2019," Oberlo, August 29, 2019, https://www.oberlo.com/blog/amazon-statistics.
2. Joe Pierre, "The Narcissism Epidemic and What We Can Do about It," *Psychology Today*, July 8, 2016, https://www.psychologytoday.com/us/blog/psych-unseen/201607/the-narcissism-epidemic-and-what-we-can-do-about-it.
3. Eric Pera, "Two Girls Face Charges in Death of Girl Who Was Bullied," *Lakeland Ledger*, October 15, 2013, https://www.theledger.com/article/LK/20131015/news/608093579/LL.

Chapter 2.1: Nine Hours a Day. Really?

1. Laura Silver, "Smartphone Ownership Is Growing Rapidly around the World, but Not Always Equally," Pew Research Center, February 5, 2019, https://www.pewresearch.org/global/2019/

02/05/smartphone-ownership-is-growing-rapidly-around-the-world-but-not-always-equally/.

2. "Time Flies: U.S. Adults Now Spend Nearly Half a Day Interacting with Media," Nielsen Media, July 31, 2018, https://www.nielsen. com/us/en/insights/article/2018/time-flies-us-adults-now-spend-nearly-half-a-day-interacting-with-media/.

3. "US Adults Now Spend 12 Hours 7 Minutes a Day Consuming Media," Emarketer, May 1, 2017, https://www.emarketer.com/ Article/US-Adults-Now-Spend-12-Hours-7-Minutes-Day-Consuming-Media/1015775.

4. Doug Smith, *[Un]Intentional: How Screens Secretly Shape Your Desires and How You Can Break Free*, (Grand Rapids, Michigan: Credo House Publishers, 2018), 2.

5. "Average Hours Per Day Spent in Selected Leisure and Sports Activities by Age," U.S. Bureau of Labor Statistics, https://www. bls.gov/charts/american-time-use/activity-leisure.htm.

6. Ibid.

7. Victoria Rideout and Michael B. Robb, "The Common Sense Census: Media Use by Tweens and Teens 2019," https://www. commonsensemedia.org/sites/default/files/uploads/research/2019-census-8-to-18-key-findings-updated.pdf.

8. "The Common Sense Census: Media Use by Kids Age Zero to Eight 2017," https://www.commonsensemedia.org/research/ the-common-sense-census-media-use-by-kids-age-zero-to-eight-2017.

Chapter 2.2: Why Screens Are Irresistible

1. Adam Alter, *Irresistible: The Rise of Addictive Technology and the Business of Keeping Us Hooked* (New York, New York: Penguin Books, 2018), 13–15.

2. Shankar Vedantam, "The Distracting Draw of Smartphones," The Hidden Brain, National Public Radio, September 6, 2019, https:// www.npr.org/2019/09/06/758199383/the-distracting-draw-of-smartphones.

3. Chavie Liever, "Tech Companies Use 'Persuasive Design' to Get Us Hooked. Psychologists Say It's Unethical," Vox, August 8, 2018,

https://www.vox.com/2018/8/8/17664580/persuasive-technology-psychology.

4. Smith, *[Un]Intentional*, 140.

Chapter 2.4: How Screens Are Conquering Youthful Rebellion

1. Jean M. Twenge, *iGen: Why Today's Super-Connected Kids Are Growing Up Less Rebellious, More Tolerant, Less Happy—and Completely Unprepared for Adulthood—and What That Means for the Rest of Us* (New York, New York: Atria Books, 2017).

2. Kate Julian, "Why Are Young People Having So Little Sex?" *The Atlantic*, December 2018, https://www.theatlantic.com/magazine/archive/2018/12/the-sex-recession/573949/.

3. Lawrence B. Finer and Jesse M. Philbin, "Trends in Ages at Key Reproductive Transitions in the United States, 1951–2010," National Institutes of Health, https://www.ncbi.nlm.nih.gov/pmc/articles/PMC4011992/.

4. "Trends in the Prevalence of Sexual Behaviors and HIV Testing National YRBS: 1991–2015," U.S. Centers for Disease Control and Prevention, https://www.cdc.gov/healthyyouth/data/yrbs/pdf/trends/2015_us_sexual_trend_yrbs.pdf.

5. Tara C. Jatlaoui et al., "Abortion Surveillance—United States, 2015," U.S. Centers for Disease Control and Prevention, https://www.cdc.gov/mmwr/volumes/67/ss/ss6713a1.htm?s_cid=ss6713a1_w.

Chapter 2.5: Sleepier, Fatter, and Sicker: What Screens Are Doing to Our Bodies

1. Connie Lin, "The Average Woman Now Weighs as Much as a 1960s Man," *Good Housekeeping*, June 16, 2015, https://www.goodhousekeeping.com/health/diet-nutrition/a32957/average-american-woman-weight/.

2. "History of Cable," California Cable & Telecommunications Association, https://www.calcable.org/learn/history-of-cable/.

3. Steven Beschloss, "Object of Interest: Remote Control," *New Yorker,* November 22, 2013, https://www.newyorker.com/tech/annals-of-technology/object-of-interest-remote-control.

4. Victoria L. Dunckley, *Reset Your Child's Brain: A Four-Week Plan to End Meltdowns, Raise Grades, and Boost Social Skills by Reversing the Effects of Electronic Screen-Time* (Novato, California: New World Library, 2015), 313.
5. Jeffrey M. Jones, "In U.S., 40 Percent Get Less Than Recommended Amount of Sleep," Gallup News, December 19, 2013, https://news.gallup.com/poll/166553/less-recommended-amount-sleep.aspx.
6. Camille Peri, "10 Things to Hate about Sleep Loss," WebMD, https://www.webmd.com/sleep-disorders/features/10-results-sleep-loss#1.
7. Carolyn Y. Johnson, "Go to Bed! Brain Researchers Warn That Lack of Sleep Is a Public Health Crisis," *Washington Post*, January 24, 2019, https://www.washingtonpost.com/national/health-science/go-to-bed-brain-researchers-warn-that-lack-of-sleep-is-a-public-health-crisis/2019/01/24/bbc61562-0a1b-11e9-85b6-41c0fe0c5b8f_story.html.
8. Michael B. Robb, "Screens and Sleep. The New Normal: Parents, Teens, Screens, and Sleep in the United States," Common Sense Media, https://www.commonsensemedia.org/sites/default/files/uploads/research/2019-new-normal-parents-teens-screens-and-sleep-united-states.pdf.
9. "What Is Computer Vision Syndrome?" WebMD, https://www.webmd.com/eye-health/computer-vision-syndrome#1.
10. Shari Rudavsky, "The Number of Nearsighted Kids Is Soaring—and the Reason Why May Not Be What You Think," *IndyStar*, December 2, 2019, https://www.indystar.com/story/news/health/2019/12/02/myopia-nearsightedness-kids-doubles-screen-use-alone-likely-not-blame/4272500002/.
11. "What You Need to Know about Gaming Injuries," *Health Essentials,* Cleveland Clinic, May 28, 2019, https://health.clevelandclinic.org/what-you-need-to-know-about-gaming-injuries/.
12. Lindsey Bever, "'Text Neck' Is Becoming an 'Epidemic' and Could Wreck Your Spine," *Washington Post*, November 19, 2014, https://www.washingtonpost.com/news/morning-mix/wp/2014/11/20/text-neck-is-becoming-an-epidemic-and-could-wreck-your-spine/.

13. Kenneth Hansraj, "Assessment of Stresses in the Cervical Spine Caused by Posture and Position of the Head," National Institutes of Health, November 25, 2014, https://www.ncbi.nlm.nih.gov/pubmed/25393825.
14. Aaron Zitner, "Working from Home Is Taking a Toll on Our Backs and Necks," *Wall Street Journal*, May 13, 2020.

Chapter 2.6: What Screens Are Doing to Our Brains

1. Sandee LaMotte, "MRIs Show Screen Time Linked to Lower Brain Development in Preschoolers," CNN, November 4, 2019, https://www.cnn.com/2019/11/04/health/screen-time-lower-brain-development-preschoolers-wellness/index.html.
2. Victoria L. Dunckley, "Gray Matters: Too Much Screen Time Damages the Brain," *Psychology Today*, February 27, 2014, https://www.psychologytoday.com/us/blog/mental-wealth/201402/gray-matters-too-much-screen-time-damages-the-brain.
3. Markham Heid, "There's Worrying New Research about Kids' Screen Time and Their Mental Health," *Time*, October 29, 2018, https://time.com/5437607/smartphones-teens-mental-health/.
4. Nicholas Kardaras, *Glow Kids* (New York, New York: Griffin Publishers, 2017), 3–4.
5. Nicholas Kardaras, "It's 'Digital Heroin': How Screens Turn Kids into Psychotic Junkies," *New York Post*, August 27, 2016, https://nypost.com/2016/08/27/its-digital-heroin-how-screens-turn-kids-into-psychotic-junkies/.
6. Rachel Bluth, "10 Percent of US Children Diagnosed with ADHD, Study Finds," CNN, August 31, 2018, https://www.cnn.com/2018/08/31/health/adhd-trends-study-partner/index.html.
7. Joshua Rosenblatt, "More Screen Time Linked to Higher Risk of ADHD in Preschool-Aged Children: Study," ABC News, April 17, 2019, https://abcnews.go.com/Health/screen-time-linked-higher-risk-adhd-preschool-aged/story?id=62429157.
8. Kardaras, *Glow Kids*, 117–19.
9. Dunckley, *Reset Your Child's Brain*, 20.

Chapter 2.7: Screens = Anxiety Machines

1. Jelena Kecmanovic, "Could Our Efforts to Avoid Anxiety Only Be Making It Worse?" *Washington Post*, July 10, 2019, https://www.washingtonpost.com/lifestyle/wellness/could-our-efforts-to-avoid-anxiety-only-be-making-it-worse/2019/07/09/df031504-91f5-11e9-aadb-74e6b2b46f6a_story.html.

2. Derek Thompson, "Why Online Dating Can Feel Like Such an Existential Nightmare," *The Atlantic*, July 21, 2019, https://www.theatlantic.com/ideas/archive/2019/07/online-dating-taking-over-everything/594337/.

3. David Brooks, "The Choice Explosion," *New York Times*, May 3, 2016, https://www.nytimes.com/2016/05/03/opinion/the-choice-explosion.html.

4. Deb Knobelman, "How to Make a Decision When You Are Afraid of Making the Wrong One," Medium.com, September 5, 2018, https://medium.com/the-ascent/how-to-make-a-decision-when-you-are-afraid-of-making-the-wrong-one-e2a27d3c89d0.

5. Joshua Rothman, "Are Things Getting Better or Worse?" *The New Yorker*, July 16, 2018, https://www.newyorker.com/magazine/2018/07/23/are-things-getting-better-or-worse.

6. Abha Bhattarai, "'It Feels Like a War Zone': As More of Them Die, Grocery Workers Increasingly Fear Showing Up at Work," *Washington Post*, April 12, 2020.

7. Chris Mooney, Brady Dennis, and Sarah Kaplan, "Hundreds of Young Americans Have Now Been Killed by the Coronavirus, Data Shows," *Washington Post*, April 8, 2020.

8. Ariana Eunjung Cha, "Young and Middle-Aged People, Barely Sick with Covid-19, Are Dying of Strokes," *Washington Post*, April 25, 2020.

9. Ryan Holmes, "We Now See 5,000 Ads A Day…and It's Getting Worse," LinkedIn blog, February 19, 2019, https://www.linkedin.com/pulse/have-we-reached-peak-ad-social-media-ryan-holmes/.

10. Meghan Blackford, "#bodypositive: A Look at Body Image & Social Media," FHE Health, November 30, 2017, https://fherehab.com/news/bodypositive/.

11. Dallas Hartwig, "The Dangers of Image Crafting," The Whole 9, http://whole9life.com/2014/03/dangers-image-crafting/.

12. Andrew Perrin and Monica Anderson, "Share of U.S. Adults Using Social Media, Including Facebook, Is Mostly Unchanged Since 2018," Pew Research Center FactTank, April 10, 2019, https://www.pewresearch.org/fact-tank/2019/04/10/share-of-u-s-adults-using-social-media-including-facebook-is-mostly-unchanged-since-2018/.

13. "Who Is More Active on Social Media? Men or Women?" Infographic on Quicksprout, April 19, 2019, https://www.quicksprout.com/who-is-more-active-on-social-media-men-or-women/.

14. Aleksandra Atanasova, "Gender-Specific Behaviors on Social Media and What They Mean for Online Communications," SocialMediaToday, November 6, 2016, https://www.socialmediatoday.com/social-networks/gender-specific-behaviors-social-media-and-what-they-mean-online-communications.

15. Moya Sarner, "The Age of Envy: How to Be Happy When Everyone Else's Life Looks Perfect," *The Guardian*, October 9, 2018, https://www.theguardian.com/lifeandstyle/2018/oct/09/age-envy-be-happy-everyone-else-perfect-social-media.

16. Rhiannon Williams, "Video Game Addiction 'Contributes to Depression and Anxiety,'" iNews.co.uk, https://inews.co.uk/news/technology/video-game-addiction-contributes-to-depression-and-anxiety-513940.

17. Gail Sullivan, "Study: More Women Than Teenage Boys Are Gamers," *Washington Post*, August 21, 2014, https://www.washingtonpost.com/news/morning-mix/wp/2014/08/22/adult-women-gamers-outnumber-teenage-boys/.

18. Anna Brown, "Younger Men Play Video Games, but So Do a Diverse Group of Other Americans," Pew Resarch Center FactTank, September 11, 2017, https://www.pewresearch.org/fact-tank/2017/09/11/younger-men-play-video-games-but-so-do-a-diverse-group-of-other-americans/.

19. Andrew Perrin, "5 Facts about Americans and Video Games," Pew Research Center FactTank, September 17, 2018, https://www.

pewresearch.org/fact-tank/2018/09/17/5-facts-about-americans-and-video-games/.

20. "U.S. Video Game Content Generated $35.4 Billion in Revenue for 2019," Entertainment Software Association press release, January 23, 2020, https://www.theesa.com/press-releases/u-s-video-game-content-generated-35-4-billion-in-revenue-for-2019/.

21. Domestic Yearly Box Office chart at Box Office Mojo, IMDb Pro, https://www.boxofficemojo.com/year/?ref_=bo_nb_di_secondarytab.

Chapter 2.8: How Screens Divide Us into Warring Tribes

1. John Gramlich, "Young Americans Are Less Trusting of Other People—and Key Institutions—Than Their Elders," Pew Research Center FactTank, August 6, 2019, https://www.pewresearch.org/fact-tank/2019/08/06/young-americans-are-less-trusting-of-other-people-and-key-institutions-than-their-elders/.

2. "Confidence in Institutions," Gallup in Depth: Topics A to Z, https://news.gallup.com/poll/1597/confidence-institutions.aspx3.

3. Jon Ronson, "When Online Shaming Goes Too Far," Ted Talk, recorded at TEDGlobalLondon, June 2015, https://www.ted.com/talks/jon_ronson_what_happens_when_online_shaming_spirals_out_of_control?language=en.

4. Darren Linvill and Patrick Warren, "That Uplifting Tweet You Just Shared? A Russian Troll Sent It," *Rolling Stone*, November 25, 2019, https://www.rollingstone.com/politics/politics-features/russia-troll-2020-election-interference-twitter-916482/#!.

5. Caitlin O'Kane, "Russian Trolls Fueled Anti-Vaccination Debate in U.S. by Spreading Misinformation on Twitter, Study Finds," CBS News, May 31, 2019, https://www.cbsnews.com/news/anti-vax-movement-russian-trolls-fueled-anti-vaccination-debate-in-us-by-spreading-misinformation-twitter-study/.

6. Thomas B. Edsall, "No Hate Left Behind," *New York Times*, March 13, 2019, https://www.nytimes.com/2019/03/13/opinion/hate-politics.html.

7. Brian Fung and Ahiza Garcia, "Facebook Has Shut Down 5.4 Billion Fake Accounts This Year," CNN, November 13, 2019,

   https://www.cnn.com/2019/11/13/tech/facebook-fake-accounts/index.html.
8. Jonathan Rausch, "Social Media, Tribalism, and the Prevalence of Fake News," Institute for Human Studies, George Mason University, BigThink series, June 12, 2019, https://theihs.org/blog/social-media-tribalism-and-the-prevalence-of-fake-news/.
9. Jane Wakefield, "Why Are People So Mean to Each Other Online?" BBC News, March 26, 2015, https://www.bbc.com/news/technology-31749753.
10. Kardaras, *Glow Kids*, 97.
11. Stephen Hawkins et al., "Hidden Tribes: A Study of America's Polarized Landscape," https://hiddentribes.us/pdf/hidden_tribes_report.pdf.

Chapter 2.9: How Screens Are Changing Communication

1. Max Roser and Estaban Ortiz-Ospina, "Literacy" Our World in Data, September 20, 2018, https://ourworldindata.org/literacy.
2. Zack Carter, "Are You Hiding behind Your Texts?" *Psychology Today*, June 27, 2017, https://www.psychologytoday.com/us/blog/clear-communication/201706/are-you-hiding-behind-your-texts.
3. Ibid.

Chapter 2.10: Swipe Left: How Screens Are Weakening Relationships

1. National Fatherhood Initiative, https://www.fatherhood.org/fatherhood-data-statistics.
2. Sandee LaMotte, "All the Lonely People: Why More of Us Will Feel Disconnected Than Ever Before," CNN Health, December 10, 2019, https://www.cnn.com/2019/12/10/health/loneliness-future-increase-wellness/index.html.
3. Jamie Ballard, "Millennials Are the Loneliest Generation" YouGov poll, July 30, 2019, https://today.yougov.com/topics/lifestyle/articles-reports/2019/07/30/loneliness-friendship-new-friends-poll-survey.

4. Sherry Amatenstein, "Not So Social Media: How Social Media Increases Loneliness," Psycom, https://www.psycom.net/how-social-media-increases-loneliness/.

5. Markham Heid, "Depression and Suicide Rates Are Rising Sharply in Young Americans, New Report Says. This May Be One Reason Why," *Time*, March 14, 2019, https://time.com/5550803/depression-suicide-rates-youth/.

6. Wikipedia, "Operation Match," https://en.wikipedia.org/wiki/Operation_Match.

7. Nancy Jo Sales, "Tinder and the Dawn of the 'Dating Apocalypse,'" *Vanity Fair*, September 2015, https://www.vanityfair.com/culture/2015/08/tinder-hook-up-culture-end-of-dating.

8. Ibid.

9. Lauren Weir, "Your Phone Is Teaching You to Pray," Gospel Coalition, January 20, 2020, https://www.thegospelcoalition.org/article/your-phone-teaching-you-pray/.

Chapter 2.11: Pornography: The Ultimate Unsafe Sex

1. Anna Pulley, "9 Surprising Reasons Why You Should Be Watching Porn," Salon, September 2, 2017, https://www.salon.com/2017/09/02/9-surprising-reasons-why-you-should-be-watching-porn_partner/.

2. "How Porn Changes the Brain," Fight the New Drug, August 23, 2017, https://fightthenewdrug.org/how-porn-changes-the-brain/.

3. Fight the New Drug, www.fightthenewdrug.org.

4. The quote in the following paragraph is from the article: "Porn's Harm Is Changing Fast," Fight the New Drug, August 23, 2017, https://fightthenewdrug.org/porns-harm-is-changing-fast/#c4.

5. M. A. Layden, (2010), "Pornography and Violence: A New look at the Research." In J. Stoner & D. Hughes (Eds.) *The Social Costs of Pornography: A Collection of Papers* (Princeton, New Jersey: Witherspoon Institute, 2010), 57–68; T. P. Kalman, "Clinical Encounters with Internet Pornography," *Journal of the American Academy of Psychoanalysis and Dynamic Psychiatry* 36, no. 4 (2008): 593– 618, doi:10.1521/jaap.2008.36.4.593.

6. "Websense Research Shows Online Pornography Sites Continue Strong Growth," PRNewswire.com, April 4, 2004.

7. "Porn More Popular Than Search," InternetWeek.com, June 4, 2004.

8. S. Negash, N. Van Ness Sheppard, N. M. Lambert, and F. D. Fincham, "Trading Later Rewards for Current Pleasure: Pornography Consumption and Delay Discounting," *Journal of Sex Research* 53, no. 6 (2016): 689–700, doi:10.1080/00224499. 2015.1025123; "Porn Sites Get More Visitors Each Month Than Netflix, Amazon, & Twitter Combined," HuffPost, May 4, 2013, http:// www.huffingtonpost.com/2013/05/03/internet-porn-stats_n_ 3187682.html.

9. W. DeKeseredy, "Critical Criminological Understandings of Adult Pornography and Women Abuse: New Progressive Directions in Research and Theory," *International Journal for Crime, Justice, and Social Democracy* 4, no. 4 (2015): 4–21, doi:10.5204/ijcjsd. v4i4.184.

10. D. Kunkel, K. Eyal, K. Finnerty, E. Biely, and E. Donnerstein, "Sex on TV 4," Menlo Park, California: Henry J. Kaiser Family Foundation, 2005.

11. Levi Lusko, "The Harmful Side Effects of Porn," XXXchurch, December 9, 2019, https://www.xxxchurch.com/men/the-harmful-side-effects-of-porn.html.

12. The quote in the following paragraph is from the article: "How Much Porn Is Healthy to Watch on the Regular?" Fight the New Drug, May 24, 2019, https://fightthenewdrug.org/ theres-no-such-thing-as-healthy-porn/.

13. Amy Fleming, "Is Porn Making Young Men Impotent?" *The Guardian*, March 11, 2019, https://www.theguardian.com/ lifeandstyle/2019/mar/11/young-men-porn-induced-erectile-dysfunction.

14. N. Doidge, *The Brain That Changes Itself* (New York, New York: Penguin Books, 2007), 102.

15. DeKeseredy, "Critical Criminological Understandings," 4–21.

16. Doidge, *The Brain That Changes Itself*, 102–3.

17. A. J. Bridges et al., "Aggression and Sexual Behavior in Best-Selling Pornography Videos: A Content Analysis Update," U.S. National

Library of Medicine, National Institutes of Health, October 16, 2010, https://www.ncbi.nlm.nih.gov/pubmed/20980228.

18. Sam Black, "Porn Is Causing Children to Sexually Assault Other Children," CovenantEyes blog post, January 9, 2020, https://www. covenanteyes.com/2020/01/09/ porn-is-causing-children-to-sexually-assault-other-children/.

19. Strange But True, "How Big Is the Porn Industry?" Medium.com, February 19, 2017, https://medium.com/@TheSBT/how-big-is-the-porn-industry-fbc1ac78091b.

20. Paul J. Wright et al., "Personal Pornography Viewing and Sexual Satisfaction: A Quadratic Analysis," *Journal of Sex & Marital Therapy* 44, no. 3 (2018): https://www.tandfonline.com/doi/full/10 .1080/0092623X.2017.1377131.

Chapter 2.12: Predators' Playground

1. Roo Powell, "I'm a 37-Year-Old Mom & I Spent Seven Days Online as an 11-Year-Old Girl. Here's What I Learned," Medium. com, December 13, 2019, https://medium.com/@sloane_ryan/ im-a-37-year-old-mom-i-spent-seven-days-online-as-an-11-year-old-girl-here-s-what-i-learned-9825e81c8e7d.

2. Roo Powell, "I'm the 37-Year-Old Who Poses as Children Online to Identify Predators: Sloane Unmasked," Medium.com, February 20, 2020, https://medium.com/@sloane_ryan/what-comes-next-sloane-unmasked-9bc5882041a3.

3. "Gemma Watts: Sex Attacks Woman Posed as Teenage Boy," BBC News, January 10, 2020, https://www.bbc.com/news/ uk-england-50985868.

4. Michael H. Keller and Gabriel J. X. Dance, "The Internet Is Overrun with Images of Child Sexual Abuse. What Went Wrong?" *New York Times*, September 29, 2019, https://www.nytimes.com/ interactive/2019/09/28/us/child-sex-abuse.html.

5. "About Alicia Kozakiewicz," The Alicia Project, http://www. aliciaproject.org/about-alicia-kozakiewicz.html.

Chapter 3.2: Be Like Mike: How to Stay Afloat

1. Ciara McCabe, "'Dopamine Fasting' Is Silicon Valley's Latest Trend. Here's What an Expert Has to Say," Science Alert, November 30, 2019, https://www.sciencealert.com/dopamine-fasting-is-silicon-valley-s-latest-trend-here-s-what-an-expert-has-to-say.

Chapter 3.3: How Excessive Eddie Cut Back

1. Adapted from the book by Adam Alter, *Irresistible: The Rise of Addictive Technology and the Business of Keeping Us Hooked* (New York, New York: Penguin Books, 2018).
2. Krissy Brady, "Is Falling Asleep with the TV on Really That Bad?" Health.com, July 16, 2018, https://www.health.com/condition/sleep/falling-asleep-tv-on.
3. Abigail Abrams, "Your Cell Phone Is 10 Times Dirtier Than a Toilet Seat. Here's What to Do about It," *Time*, August 23, 2017, https://time.com/4908654/cell-phone-bacteria/.
4. "Why Your Cellphone Has More Germs Than a Toilet," University of Arizona College of Agriculture & Life Sciences, September 15, 2012, https://cals.arizona.edu/news/why-your-cellphone-has-more-germs-toilet.
5. M. R. O'Connor, "Ditch the GPS. It's Ruining Your Brain" *Washington Post*, June 5, 2019, https://www.washingtonpost.com/opinions/ditch-the-gps-its-ruining-your-brain/2019/06/05/29a3170e-87af-11e9-98c1-e945ae5db8fb_story.html.

Chapter 3.4: Dishonorable Dan and the Poisons of the Screen World

1. Andy Greenberg, "Over 80 Percent of Dark-Web Visits Relate to Pedophilia, Study Finds," *Wired*, December 30, 2014, https://www.wired.com/2014/12/80-percent-dark-web-visits-relate-pedophilia-study-finds/.
2. "Cyber Threats and Dangers on the Deep (Dark) Web," Kaspersky Labs USA, https://usa.kaspersky.com/resource-center/threats/deep-web.

3. Jessica Seaman, "Cherry Creek High Student Who Died by Suicide Was Threatened, Encouraged to Kill Himself by 'Bullies,' Mother Alleges," *Denver Post,* April 2, 2019, https://www.denverpost.com/2019/04/02/cherry-creek-student-suicide-police-investigation/.

4. Candace McCowan, "Girl, 15, Commits Suicide after Friends Share Nude Snapchat Video Taken without Permission," WFLA-8, June 8, 2016, https://www.wfla.com/news/girl-15-commits-suicide-after-friends-share-nude-snapchat-video-taken-without-permission/.

5. "The Rise of Left-Wing, Anti-Trump Fake News," BBC, April 15, 2017, https://www.bbc.com/news/blogs-trending-39592010.

6. Helen Metella, "Lots of Sexting Can Wreck a Romance," Phys.org, January 30, 2018, https://phys.org/news/2018-01-lots-sexting-romance.html.

7. Daniella Genovese, "Sexting Study Shows Kids Starting before They Even Turn 13," Fox Business, December 18, 2019, https://www.foxbusiness.com/lifestyle/sexting-children-study.

8. K. A. Earles et al., "Media Influences on Children and Adolescents: Violence and Sex," *Journal of the National Medical Association*, September 2002, https://www.ncbi.nlm.nih.gov/pmc/articles/PMC2594155/?page=3.

9. "In Ratings Rise, Brawl's Well with Jerry Springer," *Buffalo News*, August 17, 1998, https://buffalonews.com/1998/08/18/in-ratings-rise-brawls-well-with-jerry-springer/.

10. Stuart Heritage, "Farewell to the Jerry Springer Show: 27 Years of Fights, Bleeps and Outrage," *The Guardian,* June 19, 2018, https://www.theguardian.com/tv-and-radio/2018/jun/19/farewell-to-the-jerry-springer-show-27-years-of-fights-bleeps-and-outrage.

11. Sirin Kale, "'Sometimes They're Boiled Alive': Inside the Abusive Animal Crush Industry," Vice, November 3, 2016, https://www.vice.com/en_us/article/d3gv7q/inside-abusive-animal-crush-fetish-industry.

12. Ruqayyah Moynihan, "Internet Users Access Porn Websites More Than Twitter, Wikipedia and Netflix," Business Insider, September 30, 2018, https://www.businessinsider.com/internet-users-access-porn-more-than-twitter-wikipedia-and-netflix-2018-9.

Chapter 3.5: How Albert, Dan, and Eddie Can Find Freedom

1. Damon Zahariades, *Digital Detox: The Ultimate Guide to Beating Technology Addiction, Cultivating Mindfulness, and Enjoying More Creativity, Inspiration, and Balance in Your Life!* (Amazon.com Services LLC, 2018), 123; ArtOfProductivity.com.
2. Adam Wernick, "A New Study Found People Are Terrible at Sitting Alone with Their Thoughts. How about You?" Public Radio International, July 19, 2014, https://www.pri.org/stories/2014-07-19/new-study-found-people-are-terrible-sitting-alone-their-thoughts-how-about-you.

Chapter 4.1: I'm a Parent Who Wants to Help My Kids

1. Allana Akhtar, "Bill Gates and Steve Jobs Raised Their Kids Tech-Free—and It Should've Been a Red Flag," Business Insider, September 30, 2019, https://www.businessinsider.com/screen-time-limits-bill-gates-steve-jobs-red-flag-2017-10.
2. Chris Weller, "Silicon Valley Parents Are Raising Their Kids Tech-Free—and It Should Be a Red Flag," Business Insider, February 18, 2018, https://www.businessinsider.com/silicon-valley-parents-raising-their-kids-tech-free-red-flag-2018-2.
3. Catherine Steiner-Adair, *The Big Disconnect: Protecting Childhood and Family Relationships in the Digital Age* (New York, New York: HarperCollins, 2013), 53.
4. "American Academy of Pediatrics Announces New Recommendations for Children's Media Use," American Academy of Pediatrics, October 21, 2016, https://www.aap.org/en-us/about-the-aap/aap-press-room/Pages/American-Academy-of-Pediatrics-Announces-New-Recommendations-for-Childrens-Media-Use.aspx.
5. Steiner-Adair, *The Big Disconnect*, 12.
6. Ibid., 16.

Chapter 4.3: I'm a Teacher Who Wants to Help My Students

1. Betsy Morris and Tawnell D. Hobbs, "Schools Pushed for Tech in Every Classroom. Now Parents Are Pushing Back," *Wall Street Journal*, September 3, 2019, https://www.wsj.com/articles/

in-a-school-district-where-technology-rules-grades-fall-parents-ask-why-11567523719.

2. Steiner-Adair, *The Big Disconnect*, 69.
3. Morris and Hobbs, "Schools Pushed for Tech in Every Classroom. Now Parents Are Pushing Back."
4. Tom Jacobs, "Computers in the Classroom May Do More Harm Than Good—If They're Overused," *Pacific Standard Magazine*, June 6, 2019, https://psmag.com/education/computers-in-the-classroom-may-do-more-harm-than-good.
5. Alyson Klein, "Schools Say No to Cellphones in Class. But Is It a Smart Move?" *Education Week*, September 6, 2019, https://www.edweek.org/ew/articles/2019/09/11/schools-say-no-to-cellphones-in-class.html.
6. Edward Graham, "Using Smartphones in the Classroom," National Education Association Articles & Resources, http://www.nea.org/tools/56274.htm.
7. Arnold L. Glass and Mengxue Kang (2019), "Dividing Attention in the Classroom Reduces Exam Performance," *Educational Psychology* 39, no. 3 (2019): 395–408, DOI: 10.1080/01443410.2018.1489046.

Chapter 4.4: I'm a Minister Who Wants to Help My Flock

1. David Kinnaman and Mark Matlock, *Faith for Exiles: 5 Ways for a New Generation to Follow Jesus in Digital Babylon* (Ada, Michigan: Baker Books, 2019).
2. Ian Harber, "'Progressive' Christianity: Even Shallower Than the Evangelical Faith I Left," Gospel Coalition, March 7, 2020, https://www.thegospelcoalition.org/article/progressive-christianity-shallower-evangelical-faith-i-left/.